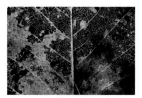

The Gospel According To Mark

COMMENTARY BY: RICK JAMES

PUBLISHED BY: CRU PRESS
THE PUBLISHING DIVISION OF THE CAMPUS MINISTRY OF CRU

CRU
100 LAKE HART DRIVE 2500 ORLANDO, FL 32832

BOOK AND COVER DESIGN: RICK JAMES AND MARK ARNOLD
WWW.ANDARNOLD.COM

SENIOR EDITOR: NEIL DOWNEY
MANUSCRIPT EDITOR: KATIE JAMES   PROOF EDITOR: JULIA WALLACE

TO ORDER GO TO WWW.CRUPRESS.COM

ISBN 1-57334-077-4

Introduction

From a grocery store aisle to a hotel room, you can find a Bible almost anywhere. But availability does not mean accessibility, and here we must be honest: as a book, the Bible is extremely difficult to understand. To read the Bible and to understand the Bible are two very different things.

This book aims to make a sincere reading and inquiry of the Bible as easy as possible. To begin with, we've narrowed the content to simply the Gospel of Mark, just one of the four Gospels and twenty-seven books of the New Testament. A digestible portion, but sufficient to understand the ministry and message of Jesus Christ.

Side notes have also been added to provide important background information: context that will clear up a considerable amount of confusion.

And last, at important junctures in the Gospel, summary explanations will serve as guides to the meaning and direction of the overall narrative.

The goal of this is not simply to know the Bible better, but to better understand the person of Christ—what he said, what he did, and who he claimed to be. We hope this approach to Mark's Gospel will serve you to that end.

About MARK

As the name would indicate, the Gospel of Mark was written by John Mark, a traveling and missionary companion to both the Apostles Peter and Paul.

Early testimony to Mark's authorship comes down to us from Papias, the Bishop of Hierapolis. Writing early in the second century, Papias states that he received the following source account of Mark's Gospel directly from the Apostle John:

"Mark, who became Peter's interpreter, wrote accurately, though not in order, all that he remembered of the things said or done by the Lord. For he had neither heard the Lord nor been one of his followers, but afterwards, as I said, he had followed Peter, who used to compose his discourses with a view to the needs of his hearers, but not as though he were drawing up a connected account of the Lord's saying . . . He was careful of this one thing, to omit none of the things he had heard and make no untrue statements therein."
—*Ecclesiastical History*, 3.39.15

As traveling companion to the Apostle Peter, the content of Mark's Gospel is largely Peter's historical account and spoken messages.

While some scholars date Mark's Gospel as early as AD 55–56, there seems to be strongest support for Mark's composition being shortly after the martyrdom of Peter, roughly AD 67.

Early church tradition locates the writing of Mark in Rome. This is consistent with the early witness that places Peter in Rome toward the end of his ministry and where he was most certainly martyred.

It is generally agreed that the Mark who accompanied both Peter and Paul and composed the Gospel, is the same John Mark sited in various places in the New Testament. The Book of Acts records his presence on the early missionary journeys (Acts 12:12, 25; Acts 13:5, 13), while both Peter and Paul include him in the closing salutations of their epistles. Paul, for example, writes to Timothy, "Get Mark and bring him with you, because he is helpful to me in my ministry" (2 Timothy 4:11).

The Gospel of Mark is a succinct, unadorned account of the ministry, suffering, death, and resurrection of Jesus. Mark 1:1 reads, "The beginning of the gospel of Jesus Christ, the Son of God." Whatever else was of pastoral concern in composing the Gospel, Mark clearly sets this forth as his thesis: Jesus is the Messiah and the Messiah is not merely a man, but the Son of God.

Israel During The Time of Jesus

PHOENICIA

ULATHA

GAULANITIS

BASHAN

AURANITIS

GALILEE

DECAPOLIS

SAMARIA

GILEAD

PERAEA

JUDAEA

IDUMAEA

AMMON

The Great Sea
(Mediterranean Sea)

Tyre
Dan
Caesarea Philippi
Ladder of Tyre
Cadasa (Kedesh)
Gischala
Seleucia
Chorazin
Bethsaida (Julias)
Ptolemais (Accho)
Magdala (Dalmanutha)
Capernaum
Tabigha
Jotapata
Cana
Gergesa
Gamala
Horns of Hattin
Tiberias
Hippos
Sepphoris
Philoteria
Abila
Nazareth
Mt. Tabor
Gadara
Plain of Esdraelon
Capitolias
Dora
Nain
Bethnabara
Pella
Caesarea
En-gannim (Ginaea)
Scythopolis (Beth-shan)
Gerasa
Samaria (Sebaste)
Mt. Ebal
Shechem
Sychar
Apollonia
Mt. Gerizim
Jacob's Well
Amathus
Antipatris
Joppa
Arimathaea (Ramathaim)
Phasaelis
Lydda (Diospolis)
Gophna
Archelais
Beth-nimrah
Philadelphia (Rabbath-ammon)
Gezer (Gazara)
Bethel
Ephraim
Ramah
Jericho
Jamnia
Emmaus
Julias (Livias, Beth-haram)
Heshbon
Ekron
Nicopolis (Emmaus)
Emmaus
Mt. of Olives
Jerusalem
Khirbet Qumran
Azotus (Ashdod)
Bethany
Ascalon
Bethlehem
Herodium
Callirhoe
Mareshah (Marisa)
Machaerus
Gaza
Hebron
Dibon
Ziph
En-gedi
Gerar
Juttah
Carmel
Masada
Rabbath Moab (Areopolis, Rabbah)
Raphia
Beersheba

Plain of Sharon
Mt. Carmel
Sea of Galilee
Wilderness of Judah
Dead Sea
ARNON

BLIND BUT NOW I SEE

JESUS' HEALING OF THE BLIND MAN (MARK 8:22–26) COMES RIGHT BEFORE PETER'S EPIPHANY AND THE TURNING POINT OF JESUS' MINISTRY. THE REASON FOR ITS PLACEMENT HERE IS THAT THE BLIND MAN SYMBOLIZES THE DISCIPLES IN THE DAWNING OF THEIR COMPREHENSION: THEY SEE JESUS, BUT VAGUELY. HOWEVER, THAT IS ABOUT TO CHANGE.

TO APPRECIATE HOW WONDERFUL THE METAPHOR OF THE BLIND MAN IS, IT'S HELPFUL TO UNDERSTAND SOMETHING ABOUT SIGHT.

WHEN WE LOOK AT AN OBJECT, THE VISUAL INFORMATION GOES TO THE BRAIN BY TWO SEPARATE PATHWAYS. ONE OF THOSE PATHWAYS IS A SHORTCUT GOING STRAIGHT TO THE FRONT OF THE BRAIN (THE PREFRONTAL CORTEX) BUT WHAT ARRIVES IS AN UNDEVELOPED PICTURE: BLOBS OF COLOR AND LIGHT—RAW, BLURRY, VISUAL DATA. A GROUP OF PEOPLE WOULD APPEAR TO BE "TREES WALKING AROUND" (MARK 8:24).

THE VISUAL INFORMATION TRAVELING ALONG THE SECOND PATHWAY IS DETOURED THROUGH THE VISUAL CORTEX, WHERE THE IMAGE IS ANALYZED AND INTERPRETED AND WHERE OUR BRAIN TELLS US WHAT WE'RE LOOKING AT. THEN IT JOINS UP WITH THE INITIAL IMPRESSION, AND THAT'S WHEN WE REALLY SEE. FIRST WE SEE VAGUELY AND THEN OUR BRAIN TELLS US WHAT WE'RE SEEING.

IN A RARE DISORDER CALLED VISUAL AGNOSIA, THE INDIVIDUAL RECEIVES THE INITIAL IMPRESSION BUT NOT THE INTERPRETATION. THE SECOND PATHWAY IS CLOSED.

THIS SEEMS TO BE THE CONDITION OF THE BLIND MAN AFTER HIS FIRST TOUCH FROM JESUS. HE HAS GONE FROM BLINDNESS TO SEEING RAW VISUAL DATA. AT THE NEUROLOGICAL LEVEL THE MAN SEES, BUT LACKS THE INTERPRETATION OF WHAT HE'S LOOKING AT.

THIS IS CERTAINLY THE PERFECT METAPHOR FOR THE DISCIPLES AT THIS POINT IN JESUS' MINISTRY. THEY SEE JESUS . . . BUT NOT REALLY. THEY RECOGNIZE HIS AUTHORITY AND POWER BUT LACK THE INTERPRETATION—THE UNDERSTANDING OF HIS TRUE IDENTITY.

WITH HIS SECOND TOUCH, JESUS IMPARTS VISUAL CLARITY TO THE BLIND MAN AND WE RIGHTLY ANTICIPATE THAT SOMETHING QUITE SIMILAR IS ABOUT TO HAPPEN TO THE DISCIPLES—THAT THEY ARE ABOUT TO RECEIVE THE INTERPRETATION AS TO JESUS' IDENTITY.

"SIMON PETER ANSWERED, 'YOU ARE THE CHRIST, THE SON OF THE LIVING GOD.' JESUS REPLIED, 'BLESSED ARE YOU, SIMON SON OF JONAH, FOR THIS WAS NOT REVEALED TO YOU BY MAN, BUT BY MY FATHER IN HEAVEN.'" (MATTHEW 16:16–17)

WHO DO PEOPLE SAY THAT I AM?

THAT I AM?

BY THIS POINT IN THE GOSPELS, TO THE KNOWING READER, JESUS' IDENTITY IS ABOUT AS VEILED AS CLARK KENT DISGUISED IN READING GLASSES, BUT TO THE DISCIPLES IT'S CLEARLY NOT SO OBVIOUS AND THERE'S A REASON WHY. THE OLD TESTAMENT CONTAINS TWO DIFFERENT AND DISTINCT PROPHETIC PORTRAITS OF THE COMING MESSIAH. ONE PORTRAYS HIM AS A POWERFUL, GLORIOUS KING, LIKE THIS DESCRIPTION FROM THE BOOK OF DANIEL:

"IN MY VISION AT NIGHT I LOOKED, AND THERE BEFORE ME WAS ONE LIKE A SON OF MAN, COMING WITH THE CLOUDS OF HEAVEN. HE APPROACHED THE ANCIENT OF DAYS AND WAS LED INTO HIS PRESENCE. HE WAS GIVEN AUTHORITY, GLORY AND SOVEREIGN POWER; ALL PEOPLES, NATIONS AND MEN OF EVERY LANGUAGE WORSHIPED HIM. HIS DOMINION IS AN EVERLASTING DOMINION THAT WILL NOT PASS AWAY, AND HIS KINGDOM IS ONE THAT WILL NEVER BE DESTROYED." (DANIEL 7:13–14)

THE OTHER DESCRIPTION OF THE MESSIAH, PARTICULARLY FOUND IN THE BOOK OF ISAIAH, PORTRAYS HIM AS A HUMBLE SERVANT, SUFFERING FOR THE SINS OF HIS PEOPLE:

"SURELY HE TOOK UP OUR INFIRMITIES AND CARRIED OUR SORROWS, YET WE CONSIDERED HIM STRICKEN BY GOD, SMITTEN BY HIM, AND AFFLICTED. BUT HE WAS PIERCED FOR OUR TRANSGRESSIONS, HE WAS CRUSHED FOR OUR INIQUITIES; THE PUNISHMENT THAT BROUGHT US PEACE WAS UPON HIM, AND BY HIS WOUNDS WE ARE HEALED. WE ALL, LIKE SHEEP, HAVE GONE ASTRAY, EACH OF US HAS TURNED TO HIS OWN WAY; AND THE LORD HAS LAID ON HIM THE INIQUITY OF US ALL." (ISAIAH 53:4–6)

EVEN IN JESUS' DAY THIS WAS AN UNRESOLVED THEOLOGICAL CONFLICT. IT WAS CLEAR THAT BOTH PORTRAITS POINTED FORWARD TO THE COMING MESSIAH, BUT HOW BOTH COULD BE TRUE OF THE SAME MESSIAH WAS A MYSTERY.

IN MARK'S GOSPEL THE TURNING POINT IS PETER'S RECOGNITION THAT JESUS IS THE CHRIST. HAVING UNDERSTOOD THAT MUCH, JESUS COULD THEN BEGIN TO EXPLAIN THE ANSWER TO THE RIDDLE: HOW THE MESSIAH COULD BE BOTH CONQUERING KING AS WELL AS A SUFFERING SERVANT.

JESUS COMBINES THE TWO PORTRAITS WITH THIS BASIC EXPLANATION: I AM THE MESSIANIC KING, BUT THE KINGDOM WILL UNFURL, NOT THROUGH MAJESTY AND POWER, BUT THROUGH HUMILITY, BROKENNESS, SUFFERING, AND DEATH. THE KINGDOM, ONCE INAUGURATED, WILL SPREAD AND GROW UNTIL THE END OF THE AGE WHEN THE SON OF MAN WILL RETURN. AND WHEN HE RETURNS IT WILL BE IN GLORY, MAJESTY, AND POWER. TWO PORTRAITS, TWO COMINGS, THE SAME MESSIAH. TO THIS DAY, THERE STILL LACKS ANOTHER PLAUSIBLE EXPLANATION FOR THESE COMPETING MESSIANIC PORTRAITS.

he rebuked Peter. "Get behind me, Satan!" he said. "You do not have in mind the things of God, but the things of men."

34 Then he called the crowd to him along with his disciples and said: "If anyone would come after me, he must deny himself and take up his cross and follow me. 35 For whoever wants to save his life will lose it, but whoever loses his life for me and for the gospel will save it. 36 What good is it for a man to gain the whole world, yet forfeit his soul? 37 Or what can a man give in exchange for his soul? 38 If anyone is ashamed of me and my words in this adulterous and sinful generation, the Son of Man will be ashamed of him when he comes in his Father's glory with the holy angels."

9 And he said to them, "I tell you the truth, some who are standing here will not taste death before they see the kingdom of God come with power."

2 After six days Jesus took Peter, James and John with him and led them up a high mountain, where they were all alone. There he was transfigured before them. 3 His clothes became dazzling white, whiter than anyone in the world could bleach them. 4 And there appeared before them Elijah and Moses, who were talking with Jesus.

GOD'S WORD

IN THE EXODUS ACCOUNT, MOSES WENT TO THE TOP OF MT. SINAI AND RETURNED WITH THE WORDS OF GOD ENGRAVED ON TABLETS. IN THIS SYMBOLIC PARALLEL, JESUS GOES TO THE MOUNTAIN TOP, BUT HERE, GOD DECLARES THE WORDS OF JESUS TO BE ONE AND THE SAME WITH HIS DIVINE COMMANDS: "THIS IS MY SON, LISTEN TO HIM." WHILE MOSES AND THE PROPHETS (SYMBOLIZED BY ELIJAH) WERE MESSENGERS OF GOD'S WORD, JESUS *IS* GOD'S WORD.

A Second Elijah

Prophesied in Hebrew Scripture was the return of the long departed prophet, Elijah, who would precede and prepare for the coming of the Messiah:

"See, I will send you the prophet Elijah before that great and dreadful day of the Lord comes." (Malachi 4:5)

Jesus explains that this prophecy about Elijah was fulfilled in the ministry of John the Baptist.

A subtle hint of this appears earlier in Mark's Gospel. As the Old Testament described Elijah wearing "a garment of hair and with a leather belt around his waist" (2 Kings 1:8), Mark points out, "John wore clothing made of camel's hair, with a leather belt around his waist" (Mark 1:6).

5 Peter said to Jesus, "Rabbi, it is good for us to be here. Let us put up three shelters—one for you, one for Moses and one for Elijah." 6 (He did not know what to say, they were so frightened.) 7 Then a cloud appeared and enveloped them, and a voice came from the cloud: "This is my Son, whom I love. Listen to him!" 8 Suddenly, when they looked around, they no longer saw anyone with them except Jesus.

9 As they were coming down the mountain, Jesus gave them orders not to tell anyone what they had seen until the Son of Man had risen from the dead. 10 They kept the matter to themselves, discussing what "rising from the dead" meant. 11 And they asked him, "Why do the teachers of the law say that Elijah must come first?" 12 Jesus replied, "To be sure, Elijah does come first, and restores all things. Why then is it written that the Son of Man must suffer much and be rejected? 13 But I tell you, Elijah has come, and they have done to him everything they wished, just as it is written about him."

14 When they came to the other disciples, they saw a large crowd around them and the teachers of the law arguing with them. 15 As soon as all the people saw Jesus, they were overwhelmed with wonder and ran to greet him. 16 "What are you arguing with them about?" he asked. 17 A man in the crowd answered, "Teacher, I brought you my son, who is possessed by a spirit that has robbed him of speech. 18 Whenever it seizes him, it throws him to the ground. He foams at the mouth, gnashes his teeth and becomes rigid. I asked your disciples to drive out the spirit, but they could not." 19 "O unbelieving generation," Jesus replied, "how long shall I stay with you? How long

shall I put up with you? Bring the boy to me." 20 So they brought him. When the spirit saw Jesus, it immediately threw the boy into a convulsion. He fell to the ground and rolled around, foaming at the mouth. 21 Jesus asked the boy's father, "How long has he been like this?" "From childhood," he answered. 22 "It has often thrown him into fire or water to kill him. But if you can do anything, take pity on us and help us." 23 " 'If you can'?" said Jesus. "Everything is possible for him who believes." 24 Immediately the boy's father exclaimed, "I do believe; help me overcome my unbelief!" 25 When Jesus saw that a crowd was running to the scene, he rebuked the evil spirit. "You deaf and mute spirit," he said, "I command you, come out of him and never enter him again." 26 The spirit shrieked, convulsed him violently and came out. The boy looked so much like a corpse that many said, "He's dead." 27 But Jesus took him by the hand and lifted him to his feet, and he stood up. 28 After Jesus had gone indoors, his disciples asked him privately, "Why couldn't we drive it out?" 29 He replied, "This kind can come out only by prayer.'"

30 They left that place and passed through Galilee. Jesus did not want anyone to know where they were, 31 because he was teaching his disciples. He said to them, "The Son of Man is going to be betrayed into the hands of men. They will kill him, and after three days he will rise." 32 But they did not understand what he meant and were afraid to ask him about it.

33 They came to Capernaum. When he was in the house, he asked them, "What were you arguing about on the road?" 34 But they kept quiet because on the way they had

WORLDLY DISCIPLES (MARK 9:14–10:16)
IN THIS SECTION OF THE GOSPEL, MARK PLACES TOGETHER FOUR STORIES OF THE DISCIPLES' FAILURE TO EXHIBIT AND EMULATE THE EXAMPLE OF JESUS: THEIR INABILITY TO RID A BOY OF AN UNCLEAN SPIRIT; THEIR ARGUMENT CONCERNING POSITION AND STATUS; THEIR COMPETITIVE ATTITUDE TOWARD THOSE OUTSIDE THEIR INNER CIRCLE; AND THEIR EXCLUSIONARY ATTITUDE TOWARD THE LITTLE CHILDREN.

IN THESE VIGNETTES WE SEE THE FULL-BLOWN HYPOCRISY OF THE PHARISEES BEGINNING TO BLOSSOM IN THE DISCIPLES. ACCORDINGLY, THIS WILL OCCUPY THE FOCUS OF JESUS' TEACHING LEADING UP TO THE CROSS.

AWAITING DEATH
WITH MOMENTUM MOVING TOWARD THE CROSS, JESUS FOCUSES HIS ATTENTION ON TEACHING, CORRECTING, AND PREPARING THE DISCIPLES FOR HIS LEAVING. ON THREE SEPARATE OCCASIONS WITHIN THIS SECTION (8:31; 9:31; 10:33) JESUS SPEAKS TO THEM ABOUT THE DEATH THAT AWAITS HIM IN JERUSALEM.

CHILD-LIKE DISCIPLES

CHILD-LIKE DOES NOT MEAN CHILDISH. LIKE A CHILD, THE DISCIPLES WERE TO REMAIN HUMBLE, TEACHABLE, DEPENDENT, AND UNSELFCONSCIOUS. AND, LIKE A CHILD, THEIR STATUS WAS TO RESIDE SOLELY IN WHO THEY REPRESENTED—JESUS.

SPIRITUAL DIVORCE

AS THE BIBLE USES THE METAPHOR OF MARRIAGE WHEN SPEAKING OF A RELATIONSHIP WITH GOD, SO HELL IS THE ULTIMATE "DIVORCE"—THE FINAL, PERMANENT SEPARATION FROM THE LOVE AND LIGHT OF GOD.

JESUS' TEACHING ON SPIRITUAL DIVORCE (HELL) IS FOLLOWED IN CONTEXT BY HIS TEACHING ON MARITAL DIVORCE (10:1–10), ITS EARTHLY ANALOG.

argued about who was the greatest. 35 Sitting down, Jesus called the Twelve and said, "If anyone wants to be first, he must be the very last, and the servant of all." 36 He took a little child and had him stand among them. Taking him in his arms, he said to them, 37 "Whoever welcomes one of these little children in my name welcomes me; and whoever welcomes me does not welcome me but the one who sent me."

38 "Teacher," said John, "we saw a man driving out demons in your name and we told him to stop, because he was not one of us." 39 "Do not stop him," Jesus said. "No one who does a miracle in my name can in the next moment say anything bad about me, 40 for whoever is not against us is for us. 41 I tell you the truth, anyone who gives you a cup of water in my name because you belong to Christ will certainly not lose his reward.

42 "And if anyone causes one of these little ones who believe in me to sin, it would be better for him to be thrown into the sea with a large millstone tied around his neck. 43 If your hand causes you to sin, cut it off. It is better for you to enter life maimed than with two hands to go into hell, where the fire never goes out. 45 And if your foot causes you to sin, cut it off. It is better for you to enter life crippled than to have two feet and be thrown into hell. 47 And if your eye causes you to sin, pluck it out. It is better for you to enter the kingdom of God with one eye than to have two eyes and be thrown into hell, 48 where " 'their worm does not die, and the fire is not quenched.' 49 Everyone will be salted with fire. 50 "Salt is good, but if it loses its saltiness, how can you make it salty again? Have salt in yourselves, and be at peace with each other."

10

Jesus then left that place and went into the region of Judea and across the Jordan. Again crowds of people came to him, and as was his custom, he taught them.

2 Some Pharisees came and tested him by asking, "Is it lawful for a man to divorce his wife?" 3 "What did Moses command you?" he replied. 4 They said, "Moses permitted a man to write a certificate of divorce and send her away." 5 "It was because your hearts were hard that Moses wrote you this law," Jesus replied. 6 "But at the beginning of creation God 'made them male and female.' 7 'For this reason a man will leave his father and mother and be united to his wife, 8 and the two will become one flesh.' So they are no longer two, but one. 9 Therefore what God has joined together, let man not separate."

10 When they were in the house again, the disciples asked Jesus about this. 11 He answered, "Anyone who divorces his wife and marries another woman commits adultery against her. 12 And if she divorces her husband and marries another man, she commits adultery."

13 People were bringing little children to Jesus to have him touch them, but the disciples rebuked them. 14 When Jesus saw this, he was indignant. He said to them, "Let the little children come to me, and do not hinder them, for the kingdom of God belongs to such as these. 15 I tell you the truth, anyone who will not receive the kingdom of God like a little child will never enter it." 16 And he took the children in his arms, put his hands on them and blessed them. 17 As Jesus started on his way, a man ran up to him and fell

MARITAL DIVORCE

WHILE LEGALISTIC IN REGARD TO THEIR OWN TRADITIONS, THE PHARISEES SEARCHED FOR LOOPHOLES IN THE LAW OF MOSES TO JUSTIFY THEIR SIN AND HYPOCRISY. THE MOST PAINED EXAMPLES WERE THE DIVORCE LAWS, WHICH ALLOWED MEN TO DIVORCE THEIR WIVES FOR THE MOST TRIVIAL OR FABRICATED OF REASONS.

JESUS CLARIFIES THAT MOSES' PERMISSION TO DIVORCE WAS A SOCIETAL ACCOMMODATION TO HUMAN WEAKNESS AND SIN. THE PHARISEES HAD MISTAKEN GOD'S TOLERANCE OF DIVORCE FOR HIS APPROVAL.

AS JOHN THE BAPTIST WAS EXECUTED FOR HIS PUBLIC CONDEMNATION OF HEROD'S ILLICIT MARRIAGE, THIS QUESTION SEEMS DESIGNED TO TRAP JESUS INTO MAKING A SIMILARLY DANGEROUS PUBLIC STATEMENT.

THE RICH MAN

WEALTH IS NOT A SIN ANY MORE THAN POVERTY IS A SIN. BUT WEALTH BLINDS ONE TO THEIR NEED FOR GOD. WEALTH, BY ITS NATURE, INHIBITS THE HUMILITY AND BROKENNESS ESSENTIAL TO FAITH AND REPENTANCE.

WITH THE RICH MAN'S MISUNDERSTANDING OF WHAT IT MEANS TO BE "GOOD" WE ARE ALERTED TO THE UNDERLYING MEANING OF THE STORY: THOSE WHO SEE THEMSELVES AS 'GOOD' (WEALTHY IN GOOD DEEDS), REMAIN IGNORANT TO THEIR NEED FOR MERCY AND FORGIVENESS.

PHYSICAL SYMBOLS TO SPIRITUAL REALITY

THE SHIFT FROM OLD COVENANT TO NEW, MARKS A SHIFT FROM OLD TESTAMENT SYMBOLS TO NEW TESTAMENT REALITY AND FULFILLMENT.

IN THE OLD TESTAMENT, FOR EXAMPLE, THE TEMPLE WAS A MAN-MADE STRUCTURE, BUILT TO HOUSE GOD'S HOLY PRESENCE; IN THE NEW TESTAMENT, BELIEVERS BECOME THE TEMPLE, EACH INDWELT BY GOD'S HOLY SPIRIT.

SIMILARLY, IN THE OLD COVENANT, MATERIAL FORTUNE WAS CONSIDERED A SIGN OF GOD'S BLESSING. HERE, JESUS DISTINGUISHES THAT THE BLESSINGS OF THE NEW COVENANT WILL BE MORE SPIRITUAL AND RELATIONAL IN NATURE. WHILE THERE IS PROMISE OF MATERIAL PROVISION, THERE IS NO PROMISE OF MATERIAL WEALTH.

on his knees before him. "Good teacher," he asked, "what must I do to inherit eternal life?" 18 "Why do you call me good?" Jesus answered. "No one is good—except God alone. 19 You know the commandments: 'Do not murder, do not commit adultery, do not steal, do not give false testimony, do not defraud, honor your father and mother.'" 20 "Teacher," he declared, "all these I have kept since I was a boy." 21 Jesus looked at him and loved him. "One thing you lack," he said. "Go, sell everything you have and give to the poor, and you will have treasure in heaven. Then come, follow me." 22 At this the man's face fell. He went away sad, because he had great wealth.

23 Jesus looked around and said to his disciples, "How hard it is for the rich to enter the kingdom of God!" 24 The disciples were amazed at his words. But Jesus said again, "Children, how hard it is to enter the kingdom of God! 25 It is easier for a camel to go through the eye of a needle than for a rich man to enter the kingdom of God." 26 The disciples were even more amazed, and said to each other, "Who then can be saved?" 27 Jesus looked at them and said, "With man this is impossible, but not with God; all things are possible with God." 28 Peter said to him, "We have left everything to follow you!" 29 "I tell you the truth," Jesus replied, "no one who has left home or brothers or sisters or mother or father or children or fields for me and the gospel 30 will fail to receive a hundred times as much in this present age (homes, brothers, sisters, mothers, children and fields—and with them, persecutions) and in the age to come, eternal life. 31 But many who are first will be last, and the last first."

32 They were on their way up to Jerusalem, with Jesus leading the way, and the disciples were astonished, while those who followed were afraid. Again he took the Twelve aside and told them what was going to happen to him. 33 "We are going up to Jerusalem," he said, "and the Son of Man will be betrayed to the chief priests and teachers of the law. They will condemn him to death and will hand him over to the Gentiles, 34 who will mock him and spit on him, flog him and kill him. Three days later he will rise."

35 Then James and John, the sons of Zebedee, came to him. "Teacher," they said, "we want you to do for us whatever we ask." 36 "What do you want me to do for you?" he asked. 37 They replied, "Let one of us sit at your right and the other at your left in your glory." 38 "You don't know what you are asking," Jesus said. "Can you drink the cup I drink or be baptized with the baptism I am baptized with?" 39 "We can," they answered. Jesus said to them, "You will drink the cup I drink and be baptized with the baptism I am baptized with, 40 but to sit at my right or left is not for me to grant. These places belong to those for whom they have been prepared." 41 When the ten heard about this, they became indignant with James and John. 42 Jesus called them together and said, "You know that those who are regarded as rulers of the Gentiles lord it over them, and their high officials exercise authority over them. 43 Not so with you. Instead, whoever wants to become great among you must be your servant, 44 and whoever wants to be first must be slave of all. 45 For even the Son of Man did not come to be served, but to serve, and to give his life as a ransom for many."

THE HISTORICITY OF MARK
THE GOSPELS INCLUDE MANY NEGATIVE, EVEN EMBARRASSING, STORIES OF THE DISCIPLES SUCH AS THESE ARGUMENTS OVER STATUS AND POSITION. AS THESE MEN BECAME THE LEADERS OF THE EARLY CHURCH, THE INCLUSION OF SUCH MATERIAL SEEMS INEXPLICABLE EXCEPT FOR A COMMITMENT TO RECORD EVENTS AS THEY ACTUALLY HAPPENED. THE ABUNDANCE OF SUCH NEGATIVE AND COUNTERPRODUCTIVE MATERIAL MAKES A STRONG CASE FOR THE ACCURACY AND HISTORICAL RELIABILITY OF THE GOSPELS.

THE STAGE IS SET

THE STAGE IS SET

MARK 10:45 SERVES AS THE CLIMAX TO THIS
SECTION, SETTING THE STAGE FOR THE PASSION
WEEK. HERE, JESUS PROVIDES THE MOST
CLARIFYING AND CONCISE DESCRIPTION OF HIS
IDENTITY AND MISSION: "THE SON OF MAN DID
NOT COME TO BE SERVED, BUT TO SERVE, AND GIVE
HIS LIFE AS A RANSOM FOR MANY." THIS IS THE
EXAMPLE OF LOVE, HUMILITY, AND SELF-SACRIFICE
THE DISCIPLES WERE TO EMULATE.

46 Then they came to Jericho. As Jesus and his disciples, together with a large crowd, were leaving the city, a blind man, Bartimaeus (that is, the Son of Timaeus), was sitting by the roadside begging. 47 When he heard that it was Jesus of Nazareth, he began to shout, "Jesus, Son of David, have mercy on me!" 48 Many rebuked him and told him to be quiet, but he shouted all the more, "Son of David, have mercy on me!" 49 Jesus stopped and said, "Call him." So they called to the blind man, "Cheer up! On your feet! He's calling you." 50 Throwing his cloak aside, he jumped to his feet and came to Jesus. 51 "What do you want me to do for you?" Jesus asked him. The blind man said, "Rabbi, I want to see." 52 "Go," said Jesus, "your faith has healed you." Immediately he received his sight and followed Jesus along the road.

11 As they approached Jerusalem and came to Bethphage and Bethany at the Mount of Olives, Jesus sent two of his disciples, 2 saying to them, "Go to the village ahead of you, and just as you enter it, you will find a colt tied there, which no one has ever ridden. Untie it and bring it here. 3 If anyone asks you, 'Why are you doing this?' tell him, 'The Lord needs it and will send it back here shortly.'" 4 They went and found a colt outside in the street, tied at a doorway. As they untied it, 5 some people standing there asked, "What are you doing, untying that colt?" 6 They answered as Jesus had told them to, and the people let them go. 7 When they brought the colt to Jesus and threw their cloaks over it, he sat on it. 8 Many people spread their cloaks on the road, while

LAST WEEK

MARK USES THEMES OTHER THAN CHRONOLOGY TO STRUCTURE THE CONTENT OF HIS GOSPEL. BUT HERE, MARK BECOMES QUITE TIME CONSCIOUS, USING DAYS AND HOURS TO MARK THE EVENTS OF JESUS' FINAL WEEK. THE WEEK BEGINS WITH JESUS' ENTRANCE INTO JERUSALEM.

IT'S SUNDAY WHEN JESUS RIDES INTO JERUSALEM ON THE BACK OF A DONKEY. UPON SEEING HIM, THE CROWDS WHO HAD GATHERED FOR THE PASSOVER BEGIN LAUDING HIM WITH PRAISE AND PALM BRANCHES. THIS ONLY CONFIRMS TO THE RELIGIOUS LEADERS THE NECESSITY OF THEIR PLAN TO KILL JESUS, AND THE NEED FOR BOTH SECRECY AND HASTE. ON MONDAY AND TUESDAY HOSTILITIES ERUPT BETWEEN JESUS AND THE RELIGIOUS LEADERS, BUT IT'S STILL CONFINED TO VERBAL SPARRING. IN ALL OF THE GOSPELS, WEDNESDAY IS PASSED OVER IN SILENCE—A DEEP INHALE IN THE TENSION.

ON THURSDAY EVENING, JESUS CELEBRATES PASSOVER IN WHAT WILL BE HIS LAST SUPPER WITH THE DISCIPLES. AFTER THE MEAL THEY WALK TO THE GARDEN OF GETHSEMANE, WHERE JESUS SPENDS HIS FINAL HOURS IN AGONIZED PRAYER. IT'S HERE AT GETHSEMANE THAT JESUS IS TAKEN INTO CUSTODY. THROUGH THURSDAY NIGHT AND INTO FRIDAY MORNING, JESUS IS DRAGGED THROUGH THREE MOCK TRIALS: ONE BEFORE THE RELIGIOUS LEADERS OF THE SANHEDRIN; A CIVIL TRIAL BEFORE HEROD, THE POLITICAL KING OF ISRAEL; AND THEN FINALLY A THIRD TRIAL BEFORE THE ROMAN GOVERNOR PONTIUS PILATE. (AS AN OCCUPIED NATION, ONLY ROME COULD CONFER A SENTENCE OF CAPITAL PUNISHMENT.)

FRIDAY AFTERNOON, JESUS IS CRUCIFIED. HIS BODY IS TAKEN DOWN AND LAID IN A TOMB EARLY FRIDAY EVENING. ON SUNDAY COMES THE NEWS THAT THE TOMB IS EMPTY AND THE REPORTS THAT JESUS IS ALIVE.

MESSIAH'S ARRIVAL FORETOLD

IN THE OLD TESTAMENT BOOK OF ZECHARIAH, DATING BACK FIVE
HUNDRED YEARS BEFORE CHRIST, THERE IS A SPECIFIC PROPHECY
CONCERNING THE FUTURE MESSIAH: WHEN HE ARRIVED IN
JERUSALEM HE WOULD STAND UPON THE MOUNT OF OLIVES AND
CLEANSE THE TEMPLE OF ITS MORAL AND SPIRITUAL CORRUPTION:

*"ON THAT DAY HIS FEET WILL STAND ON THE MOUNT OF OLIVES,
EAST OF JERUSALEM . . . AND ON THAT DAY THERE WILL NO LONGER
BE A TRADER IN THE HOUSE OF THE LORD ALMIGHTY."*
(ZECHARIAH 14:4, 21 ESV)

IN JESUS' ACTIONS, THE PROPHECY IS QUITE LITERALLY FULFILLED.

others spread branches they had cut in the fields. 9 Those who went ahead and those who followed shouted,

"Hosanna!'"

"Blessed is he who comes in the name of the Lord!"

10   "Blessed is the coming kingdom of our father David!"

"Hosanna in the highest!"

11 Jesus entered Jerusalem and went to the temple. He looked around at everything, but since it was already late, he went out to Bethany with the Twelve. 12 The next day as they were leaving Bethany, Jesus was hungry. 13 Seeing in the distance a fig tree in leaf, he went to find out if it had any fruit. When he reached it, he found nothing but leaves, because it was not the season for figs. 14 Then he said to the tree, "May no one ever eat fruit from you again." And his disciples heard him say it.

15 On reaching Jerusalem, Jesus entered the temple area and began driving out those who were buying and selling there. He overturned the tables of the money changers and the benches of those selling doves, 16 and would not allow anyone to carry merchandise through the temple courts. 17 And as he taught them, he said, "Is it not written:

" 'My house will be called a house of prayer for all nations'?

But you have made it 'a den of robbers.'"

18 The chief priests and the teachers of the law heard this and began looking for a way

JESUS ENTERS JERUSALEM
THE ENTRANCE INTO JERUSALEM MARKS THE LAST STAGE OF JESUS' MINISTRY. IN A MILITARY CUSTOM OF THE PERIOD, A CONQUERING KING WOULD APPROACH A NATION RIDING UPON A DONKEY IF TERMS OF PEACE WERE BEING OFFERED, AS IS THE CASE HERE. IF CONQUEST WAS THE INTENTION, THE KING WOULD RIDE IN ON A WHITE STALLION, WHICH IS HOW JESUS IS PICTURED IN THE BOOK OF REVELATION AT HIS SECOND COMING:

"I SAW HEAVEN STANDING OPEN AND THERE BEFORE ME WAS A WHITE HORSE, WHOSE RIDER IS CALLED FAITHFUL AND TRUE. WITH JUSTICE HE JUDGES AND MAKES WAR." (REVELATION 19:11)

FRUITLESS ISRAEL

IN HEBREW SCRIPTURE THE FIG TREE WAS OFTEN A SYMBOL FOR THE NATION OF ISRAEL. JESUS FINDING NO FIGS ON THE FIG TREE IS SYNONYMOUS WITH HIS FINDING NO WORSHIP OR SPIRITUAL FRUIT IN ISRAEL'S TEMPLE.

JESUS EMPHASIZED THE TEMPLE BEING A "HOUSE OF PRAYER FOR ALL NATIONS" BECAUSE THE COURT OF THE GENTILES WAS BEING USED AS THE MONEY EXCHANGE. THIS WAS THE ONE LOCATION WITHIN THE JERUSALEM TEMPLE WHERE ANY FOREIGNER OR GENTILE COULD COME AND WORSHIP GOD.

JUDGEMENT PRONOUNCED

CURSING THE FIG TREE AND DRIVING OUT THE MONEYCHANGERS WERE SYMBOLIC ACTS: A PHYSICAL DEMONSTRATION, OR ENACTED PROPHECY, OF COMING JUDGMENT UPON ISRAEL. IN AD 70 THE TEMPLE WOULD BE DESTROYED BY ROME—EVERY LAST STONE THROWN DOWN—AND THE JEWS WOULD BE DRIVEN OUT, NOT TO RETURN TO THEIR HOMELAND FOR ANOTHER NINETEEN HUNDRED YEARS (1948).

to kill him, for they feared him, because the whole crowd was amazed at his teaching. 19 When evening came, they went out of the city.

20 In the morning, as they went along, they saw the fig tree withered from the roots. 21 Peter remembered and said to Jesus, "Rabbi, look! The fig tree you cursed has withered!" 22 "Have faith in God," Jesus answered. 23 "I tell you the truth, if anyone says to this mountain, 'Go, throw yourself into the sea,' and does not doubt in his heart but believes that what he says will happen, it will be done for him. 24 Therefore I tell you, whatever you ask for in prayer, believe that you have received it, and it will be yours. 25 And when you stand praying, if you hold anything against anyone, forgive him, so that your Father in heaven may forgive you your sins.'"

27 They arrived again in Jerusalem, and while Jesus was walking in the temple courts, the chief priests, the teachers of the law and the elders came to him. 28 "By what authority are you doing these things?" they asked. "And who gave you authority to do this?" 29 Jesus replied, "I will ask you one question. Answer me, and I will tell you by what authority I am doing these things. 30 John's baptism—was it from heaven, or from men? Tell me!" 31 They discussed it among themselves and said, "If we say, 'From heaven,' he will ask, 'Then why didn't you believe him?' 32 But if we say, 'From men' . . . .'" (They feared the people, for everyone held that John really was a prophet.) 33 So they answered Jesus, "We don't know." Jesus said, "Neither will I tell you by what authority I am doing these things."

12 He then began to speak to them in parables: "A man planted a vineyard. He put a wall around it, dug a pit for the winepress and built a watchtower. Then he rented the vineyard to some farmers and went away on a journey. 2 At harvest time he sent a servant to the tenants to collect from them some of the fruit of the vineyard. 3 But they seized him, beat him and sent him away empty-handed. 4 Then he sent another servant to them; they struck this man on the head and treated him shamefully. 5 He sent still another, and that one they killed. He sent many others; some of them they beat, others they killed. 6 "He had one left to send, a son, whom he loved. He sent him last of all, saying, 'They will respect my son.' 7 "But the tenants said to one another, 'This is the heir. Come, let's kill him, and the inheritance will be ours.' 8 So they took him and killed him, and threw him out of the vineyard. 9 "What then will the owner of the vineyard do? He will come and kill those tenants and give the vineyard to others. 10 Haven't you read this scripture:

> " 'The stone the builders rejected
>
>   has become the capstone;
>
> 11   the Lord has done this,
>
>   and it is marvelous in our eyes'?"

12 Then they looked for a way to arrest him because they knew he had spoken the parable against them. But they were afraid of the crowd; so they left him and went away. 13 Later they sent some of the Pharisees and Herodians to Jesus to catch him in

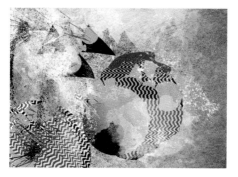

PARABLE OF THE VINEYARD
IN THE PARABLE, THE VINEYARD REPRESENTS ISRAEL. JESUS USES IT TO REHEARSE ISRAEL'S LONG HISTORY OF DEFIANCE IN RESPONSE TO THE PROPHETS SENT TO HER, MANY OF WHOM WERE KILLED AT THE HANDS OF ISRAEL'S LEADERS. AND NOW, AS THE PARABLE INFERS, THEY WERE PLOTTING THE DEATH OF GOD'S OWN SON. THIS PARABLE IS YET ANOTHER WARNING OF JUDGMENT SHOULD ISRAEL FAIL TO TURN FROM HER COURSE OF UNBELIEF.

SETTING A TRAP

IN ATTEMPTING TO TRAP JESUS, THE PHARISEES
TRIED TO PLACE HIM ON THE HORNS OF A DILEMMA.
IF JESUS HAD SAID "DON'T PAY TAXES" THEN HE
WOULD HAVE BEEN SUBJECT TO ROMAN ARREST AND
EXECUTION; IF HE HAD SAID TO "PAY TAXES," HE
WOULD HAVE ALIENATED THE JEWISH CROWDS THAT
SAW ROMAN OCCUPATION AS AN AFFRONT TO GOD.

LIBERAL SADDUCEES

NOT ALL IN ISRAEL'S RELIGIOUS COMMUNITY
WERE CONSERVATIVES AND FUNDAMENTALISTS.
THE SADDUCEES WERE THE LIBERAL,
PROGRESSIVE PARTY: THEIR AMBITIONS FOR
JUDAISM MORE POLITICAL THAN SPIRITUAL.
AS A PROGRESSIVE MOVEMENT, THEY WERE
DRIVEN BY A VISION FOR THE STATE MORE
THAN THE AFTERLIFE. JESUS' OPINION OF
THEM IS NO HIGHER THAN HIS REGARD FOR
THE PHARISEES. THEIR ERROR SPRANG FROM
NOT KNOWING OR BELIEVING IN THE REALITY
AND REVELATION OF GOD.

his words. 14 They came to him and said, "Teacher, we know you are a man of integrity. You aren't swayed by men, because you pay no attention to who they are; but you teach the way of God in accordance with the truth. Is it right to pay taxes to Caesar or not? 15 Should we pay or shouldn't we?" But Jesus knew their hypocrisy. "Why are you trying to trap me?" he asked. "Bring me a denarius and let me look at it." 16 They brought the coin, and he asked them, "Whose portrait is this? And whose inscription?" "Caesar's," they replied. 17 Then Jesus said to them, "Give to Caesar what is Caesar's and to God what is God's." And they were amazed at him.

18 Then the Sadducees, who say there is no resurrection, came to him with a question. 19 "Teacher," they said, "Moses wrote for us that if a man's brother dies and leaves a wife but no children, the man must marry the widow and have children for his brother. 20 Now there were seven brothers. The first one married and died without leaving any children. 21 The second one married the widow, but he also died, leaving no child. It was the same with the third. 22 In fact, none of the seven left any children. Last of all, the woman died too. 23 At the resurrection whose wife will she be, since the seven were married to her?"

24 Jesus replied, "Are you not in error because you do not know the Scriptures or the power of God? 25 When the dead rise, they will neither marry nor be given in marriage; they will be like the angels in heaven. 26 Now about the dead rising—have you not read in the book of Moses, in the account of the bush, how God said to him, 'I am the God of Abraham, the God of Isaac, and the God of Jacob'? 27 He is not the

God of the dead, but of the living. You are badly mistaken!"

28 One of the teachers of the law came and heard them debating. Noticing that Jesus had given them a good answer, he asked him, "Of all the commandments, which is the most important?" 29 "The most important one," answered Jesus, "is this: 'Hear, O Israel, the Lord our God, the Lord is one. 30 Love the Lord your God with all your heart and with all your soul and with all your mind and with all your strength.' 31 The second is this: 'Love your neighbor as yourself.' There is no commandment greater than these." 32 "Well said, teacher," the man replied. "You are right in saying that God is one and there is no other but him. 33 To love him with all your heart, with all your understanding and with all your strength, and to love your neighbor as yourself is more important than all burnt offerings and sacrifices." 34 When Jesus saw that he had answered wisely, he said to him, "You are not far from the kingdom of God." And from then on no one dared ask him any more questions.

35 While Jesus was teaching in the temple courts, he asked, "How is it that the teachers of the law say that the Christ is the son of David? 36 David himself, speaking by the Holy Spirit, declared:

"'The Lord said to my Lord:

"Sit at my right hand until I put your enemies under your feet.'"

37 David himself calls him 'Lord.' How then can he be his son?" The large crowd listened to him with delight.

ON THE GREATEST COMMANDMENT
THE PHARISEES ENDLESSLY DEBATED WHICH OF THE LAW'S COMMANDMENTS WAS THE 'HEAVIER' OR 'GREATEST.' WHILE ASKED FOR ONLY ONE COMMANDMENT, JESUS COMBINES TWO IN HIS ANSWER (LEVITICUS 19:34; DEUTERONOMY 6:5). IN DOING SO, JESUS IS TEACHING THAT LOVE FOR GOD AND LOVE FOR NEIGHBOR ARE INSEPARABLE. THE CLAIM TO LOVE GOD IS VERIFIED BY A LOVE FOR ONE'S NEIGHBOR.

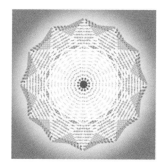

KING DAVID VS. KING MESSIAH

GOD'S SON IS ABOVE ANY OF GOD'S SERVANTS, EVEN DAVID. THIS POINT OF CLARIFICATION WAS CRUCIAL: THOSE EXPECTING THE MESSIAH TO BE MERELY A CHARISMATIC LEADER—SOMEONE LIKE KING DAVID—WOULD NEVER RECOGNIZE HIM, EVEN IF HE WERE IN THEIR MIDST. WHICH, OF COURSE, HE WAS.

SPEAKING TO GOD'S CHOICE OF DAVID OVER SAUL FOR KING OF ISRAEL, 1 SAMUEL 16:7 STATES THAT "PEOPLE LOOK AT THE OUTWARD APPEARANCE, BUT THE LORD LOOKS AT THE HEART." HERE, AMONG THE THRONGS MILLING ABOUT THE TEMPLE, JESUS DISCERNS THE HEART OF A TRUE WORSHIPPER, AND THE COMPARISON BETWEEN DAVID AND THE MESSIAH BECOMES ACUTE: WHILE DAVID HAD A HEART FOR GOD, JESUS IS THE ONE WHO SEARCHES HEARTS.

38 As he taught, Jesus said, "Watch out for the teachers of the law. They like to walk around in flowing robes and be greeted in the marketplaces, 39 and have the most important seats in the synagogues and the places of honor at banquets. 40 They devour widows' houses and for a show make lengthy prayers. Such men will be punished most severely."

41 Jesus sat down opposite the place where the offerings were put and watched the crowd putting their money into the temple treasury. Many rich people threw in large amounts. 42 But a poor widow came and put in two very small copper coins, worth only a fraction of a penny. 43 Calling his disciples to him, Jesus said, "I tell you the truth, this poor widow has put more into the treasury than all the others. 44 They all gave out of their wealth; but she, out of her poverty, put in everything—all she had to live on."

13 As he was leaving the temple, one of his disciples said to him, "Look, Teacher! What massive stones! What magnificent buildings!" 2 "Do you see all these great buildings?" replied Jesus. "Not one stone here will be left on another; every one will be thrown down." 3 As Jesus was sitting on the Mount of Olives opposite the temple, Peter, James, John and Andrew asked him privately, 4 "Tell us, when will these things happen? And what will be the sign that they are all about to be fulfilled?" 5 Jesus said to them: "Watch out that no one deceives you. 6 Many will come in my name, claiming,

'I am he,' and will deceive many. 7 When you hear of wars and rumors of wars, do not be alarmed. Such things must happen, but the end is still to come. 8 Nation will rise against nation, and kingdom against kingdom. There will be earthquakes in various places, and famines. These are the beginning of birth pains.

9 "You must be on your guard. You will be handed over to the local councils and flogged in the synagogues. On account of me you will stand before governors and kings as witnesses to them. 10 And the gospel must first be preached to all nations. 11 Whenever you are arrested and brought to trial, do not worry beforehand about what to say. Just say whatever is given you at the time, for it is not you speaking, but the Holy Spirit. 12 "Brother will betray brother to death, and a father his child. Children will rebel against their parents and have them put to death. 13 All men will hate you because of me, but he who stands firm to the end will be saved.

14 "When you see 'the abomination that causes desolation' standing where it does not belong—let the reader understand—then let those who are in Judea flee to the mountains. 15 Let no one on the roof of his house go down or enter the house to take anything out. 16 Let no one in the field go back to get his cloak. 17 How dreadful it will be in those days for pregnant women and nursing mothers! 18 Pray that this will not take place in winter, 19 because those will be days of distress unequaled from the beginning, when God created the world, until now—and never to be equaled again. 20 If the Lord had not cut short those days, no one would survive. But for the sake of the elect, whom

THE TRUE TEMPLE
THE TEMPLE IN JERUSALEM WAS THE SPIRITUAL CENTER OF ISRAEL. IN JEWISH WORSHIP, IT WAS THE TEMPLE THAT HOUSED THE VERY PRESENCE OF GOD, AND WAS THE UNIQUE LOCATION OF HIS DWELLING AMONG MAN. AS SUCH, THE TEMPLE SYMBOLIZED AND POINTED TO JESUS, WHO WAS THE EMBODIMENT OF GOD: GOD'S PRESENCE, DWELLING AMONG US.

IN SPEAKING OF THE TEMPLE'S DESTRUCTION, THEN, JESUS IS ALSO FORESHADOWING HIS OWN DEATH.

A SECOND COMING
JEWISH EXPECTATION WAS THAT THE COMING MESSIAH WOULD USHER IN THE END OF THE AGE. AS JESUS PREPARES HIS DISCIPLES FOR HIS COMING DEATH, QUESTIONS AND CONFUSION CONCERNING THE END OF THE AGE ARE ADDRESSED AND CLARIFIED: IT WILL BE JESUS' RETURN, OR SECOND COMING, THAT WILL BRING THIS AGE TO A CLOSE AND INAUGURATE THE VISIBLE REIGN OF CHRIST ON EARTH.

THE SON OF MAN

MORE THAN ANY TITLE, JESUS USED THE TERM "SON OF MAN." IT'S LIKELY HE AVOIDED THE LABEL OF "MESSIAH" DUE TO MISCONCEPTIONS ISRAEL HAD ATTACHED TO IT. THE SON OF MAN DESIGNATION COMES FROM THE BOOK OF DANIEL WHERE IT'S USED TO DESCRIBE THIS MESSIANIC FIGURE:

"IN MY VISION AT NIGHT I LOOKED, AND THERE BEFORE ME WAS ONE LIKE A SON OF MAN, COMING WITH THE CLOUDS OF HEAVEN . . . HE WAS GIVEN AUTHORITY, GLORY AND SOVEREIGN POWER; ALL PEOPLES, NATIONS AND MEN OF EVERY LANGUAGE WORSHIPED HIM. HIS DOMINION IS AN EVERLASTING DOMINION THAT WILL NOT PASS AWAY, AND HIS KINGDOM IS ONE THAT WILL NEVER BE DESTROYED." (DANIEL 7:13–14)

AS THIS DESCRIPTION MAKES CLEAR, THE "SON OF MAN" TITLE CARRIED WITH IT A CLAIM BEYOND POPULAR AND POLITICAL EXPECTATIONS.

he has chosen, he has shortened them. 21 At that time if anyone says to you, 'Look, here is the Christ !' or, 'Look, there he is!' do not believe it. 22 For false Christs and false prophets will appear and perform signs and miracles to deceive the elect—if that were possible. 23 So be on your guard; I have told you everything ahead of time.

24 "But in those days, following that distress,

"'the sun will be darkened,

and the moon will not give its light;

25   the stars will fall from the sky,

and the heavenly bodies will be shaken.'

26 "At that time men will see the Son of Man coming in clouds with great power and glory. 27 And he will send his angels and gather his elect from the four winds, from the ends of the earth to the ends of the heavens.

28 "Now learn this lesson from the fig tree: As soon as its twigs get tender and its leaves come out, you know that summer is near. 29 Even so, when you see these things happening, you know that it is near, right at the door. 30 I tell you the truth, this generation will certainly not pass away until all these things have happened. 31 Heaven and earth will pass away, but my words will never pass away.

32 "No one knows about that day or hour, not even the angels in heaven, nor the Son, but only the Father. 33 Be on guard! Be alert ! You do not know when that time will come.

34 It's like a man going away: He leaves his house and puts his servants in charge, each with his assigned task, and tells the one at the door to keep watch. 35 "Therefore keep watch because you do not know when the owner of the house will come back—whether in the evening, or at midnight, or when the rooster crows, or at dawn. 36 If he comes suddenly, do not let him find you sleeping. 37 What I say to you, I say to everyone: 'Watch!'"

14 Now the Passover and the Feast of Unleavened Bread were only two days away, and the chief priests and the teachers of the law were looking for some sly way to arrest Jesus and kill him. 2 "But not during the Feast," they said, "or the people may riot."

3 While he was in Bethany, reclining at the table in the home of a man known as Simon the Leper, a woman came with an alabaster jar of very expensive perfume, made of pure nard. She broke the jar and poured the perfume on his head. 4 Some of those present were saying indignantly to one another, "Why this waste of perfume? 5 It could have been sold for more than a year's wages and the money given to the poor." And they rebuked her harshly. 6 "Leave her alone," said Jesus. "Why are you bothering her? She has done a beautiful thing to me. 7 The poor you will always have with you, and you can help them any time you want. But you will not always have me. 8 She did what she could. She poured perfume on my body beforehand to prepare for my burial. 9 I tell you

THE PASSION NARRATIVE (MARK 14:1-16:8)
THE GROWING ANIMOSITY BETWEEN JESUS AND THE RELIGIOUS ESTABLISHMENT COMES TO A CLIMAX IN THE PASSION AND RESURRECTION ACCOUNT. THESE EVENTS OF JESUS' MINISTRY WERE THE VERY FIRST TO BE WRITTEN DOWN AND CIRCULATED. THESE EARLY WRITTEN TRADITIONS WERE INCORPORATED, SOMETIMES WORD-FOR-WORD, INTO THE GOSPELS OF MATTHEW, MARK, AND LUKE, AND ARE RESPONSIBLE FOR SIMILAR PHRASING BETWEEN THEM.

THE EXTRAVAGANT LOVE OF GOD
THE ACTIONS OF THE WOMAN HOLD SYMBOLIC AS WELL AS PROPHETIC SIGNIFICANCE. THE BREAKING OF THE JAR AND POURING OUT OF THE FRAGRANCE SIGNIFIES THE DEATH OF CHRIST: THE BREAKING OF HIS BODY AND POURING OUT OF HIS LIFE. TO THE SKEPTIC, JESUS' DEATH COULD SEEM LIKE THE ALABASTER JAR—A MEANINGLESS WASTE. BUT IT WAS AN EXTRAVAGANT EXPRESSION OF GOD'S LOVE, MERCY, AND GRACE, EXEMPLIFIED IN THE WOMAN'S SACRIFICE.

IT IS IMPORTANT TO VIEW SUCH SYMBOLIC EVENTS, NOT AS ALLEGORY OR LITERARY DEVICE, BUT AS REAL EVENTS WITH OBSERVABLE IRONY.

SO WHY DID JESUS HAVE TO DIE? IT'S IMPORTANT TO ACKNOWLEDGE THAT THE REALITY, THE ACTUAL "WHY," IS FAR DEEPER THAN ANY ANSWER PACKAGED FOR HUMAN COMPREHENSION. IT'S LIKE BEING ASKED BY A LOVED ONE: "WHY DO YOU LOVE ME?" THERE ARE CERTAINLY SOME THINGS THAT CAN AND SHOULD BE SAID, BUT THE TRUTH IS UNIMAGINABLY COMPLEX AND COULD NEVER FIND ADEQUATE VERBAL EXPRESSION. HERE, AT LEAST, IS WHAT CAN AND SHOULD BE SAID ABOUT THE DEATH OF JESUS:

IF YOU WERE TO READ THROUGH THE BIBLE, COVER-TO-COVER, THREE THINGS ABOUT GOD'S CHARACTER WOULD IMPRESS UPON YOUR MIND: GOD IS LOVING (KIND, FAITHFUL, FORGIVING, MERCIFUL, ETC.); GOD IS JUST (THEREFORE THE WICKED ARE NOT EXCUSED OR IGNORED); AND GOD IS HOLY.

LOVING AND JUST ARE SELF-EXPLANATORY, BUT TO BETTER PICTURE WHAT HOLINESS IS, THE BIBLE USES AN UNEXPECTED WORD-PICTURE TO DESCRIBE THE REACTION WHEN GOD'S HOLINESS COMES IN CONTACT WITH SIN AND EVIL. THAT WORD IS "VOMIT" (LEVITICUS 20:22; PSALM 95:10; REVELATION 3:16). IF YOU WERE TO DRINK POISON, YOUR BODY WOULD BEGIN TO CONVULSE AND YOU'D MOST LIKELY VOMIT WHAT YOU INGESTED: SUCH IS THE BODY'S NATURAL REACTION TO WHAT IT FINDS POISONOUS TO ITSELF. AND THUS THE BIBLICAL WORD-PICTURE: THIS CONVULSING REACTION IS WHAT HAPPENS WHEN A BEING OF PURE LIGHT AND LIFE ENCOUNTERS HUMAN EVIL.

THE PROBLEM, AND A SERIOUS ONE, IS THAT WE ARE ALL FILLED WITH EVIL THOUGHTS, AMBITIONS, AND DESIRES. TO ILLUSTRATE THIS POINT, AT THIS VERY MOMENT I COUNT TWENTY-SIX WARS GOING ON IN THE WORLD, ALONG WITH GENOCIDE AND OTHER ATROCITIES OF WHICH WE ARE BOTH AWARE.

AND SO HERE ARE THE CONTOURS OF THE DILEMMA THAT PRECIPITATE THE DEATH OF CHRIST. GOD TRULY DOES LOVE US. BUT GOD IS JUST AS WELL AS HOLY, AND THEREFORE SIN IS AN ENORMOUS OBSTACLE BETWEEN GOD AND US. FOR GOD TO IGNORE EVIL HE WOULD HAVE TO CEASE TO BE GOD—CHANGING HIS VERY NATURE. GOD, WHILE POSSESSING ALL THE ATTRIBUTES OF LOVE, JUSTICE, PURITY, AND HOLINESS, IS NEVER IN CONFLICT WITH HIMSELF, AND EVERYTHING HE DOES IS CONSISTENT WITH ALL THAT HE IS. IT IS IN CHRIST'S DEATH THAT GOD IS ABLE TO SIMULTANEOUSLY LOVE AND FORGIVE US, WHILE DESTROYING EVIL AND SIN. AS THE SCRIPTURES PHRASE THIS BOTTOMLESS MYSTERY, "GOD MADE HIM WHO HAD NO SIN TO BE SIN FOR US, SO THAT IN HIM WE MIGHT BECOME THE RIGHTEOUSNESS OF GOD" (2 CORINTHIANS 5:21).

PERHAPS THIS IS TOO ABSTRACT. IF WE WERE TO TRY TO PUT IT INTO SIMPLER LANGUAGE WE MIGHT USE THE WORDS OF PHILOSOPHER PETER KREEFT:

"ALL SIN IS SPIRITUAL GARBAGE, AND NECESSARILY MEETS ITS END IN DESTRUCTION. GOD CAN'T LET GARBAGE INTO HEAVEN. ONLY IF THE 'SINNER' WON'T LET GO OF HIS GARBAGE DOES HE GET BURNED WITH IT. GOD OFFERS TO TAKE THE GARBAGE OFF HIS BACK, TO SEPARATE THE 'SINNER' FROM THE SIN SO THAT THE SINNER IS NOT SEPARATED FROM GOD. JESUS IS THE GARBAGE MAN."

THIS, IN EFFECT, IS WHAT JESUS SAID WHEN HE DECLARED, "THE SON OF MAN DID NOT COME TO BE SERVED, BUT TO SERVE, AND GIVE HIS LIFE AS A RANSOM FOR MANY" (MARK 10:45).

YOU MIGHT EXPECT THE REDEMPTION OF HUMANKIND TO BE MORE PALATABLE, AND INSTEAD HERE WE ARE LOOKING AT A REJECTED MESSIAH, TORTURED BEYOND RECOGNITION, GIVING HIS LIFE FOR OURS. BUT GOD CHOSE THIS APPARENT IRONY AND FOOLISHNESS TO BE THE MOST FITTING VEHICLE FOR THE REDEMPTION OF A TERMINALLY FAITHLESS AND PRIDEFUL HUMANITY. THE APOSTLE PAUL OFFERS THAT DISCLAIMER IN HIS LETTER TO THE CORINTHIANS:

"SINCE IN THE WISDOM OF GOD THE WORLD THROUGH ITS WISDOM DID NOT KNOW HIM, GOD WAS PLEASED THROUGH THE FOOLISHNESS OF WHAT WAS PREACHED TO SAVE THOSE WHO BELIEVE. JEWS DEMAND MIRACULOUS SIGNS AND GREEKS LOOK FOR WISDOM, BUT WE PREACH CHRIST CRUCIFIED: A STUMBLING BLOCK TO JEWS AND FOOLISHNESS TO GENTILES. … FOR THE FOOLISHNESS OF GOD IS WISER THAN MAN'S WISDOM, AND THE WEAKNESS OF GOD IS STRONGER THAN MAN'S STRENGTH." (1 CORINTHIANS 1:21–23, 25)

the truth, wherever the gospel is preached throughout the world, what she has done will also be told, in memory of her."

10 Then Judas Iscariot, one of the Twelve, went to the chief priests to betray Jesus to them. 11 They were delighted to hear this and promised to give him money. So he watched for an opportunity to hand him over.

12 On the first day of the Feast of Unleavened Bread, when it was customary to sacrifice the Passover lamb, Jesus' disciples asked him, "Where do you want us to go and make preparations for you to eat the Passover?" 13 So he sent two of his disciples, telling them, "Go into the city, and a man carrying a jar of water will meet you. Follow him. 14 Say to the owner of the house he enters, 'The Teacher asks: Where is my guest room, where I may eat the Passover with my disciples?' 15 He will show you a large upper room, furnished and ready. Make preparations for us there." 16 The disciples left, went into the city and found things just as Jesus had told them. So they prepared the Passover.

17 When evening came, Jesus arrived with the Twelve. 18 While they were reclining at the table eating, he said, "I tell you the truth, one of you will betray me—one who is eating with me." 19 They were saddened, and one by one they said to him, "Surely not I?" 20 "It is one of the Twelve," he replied, "one who dips bread into the bowl with me. 21 The Son of Man will go just as it is written about him. But woe to that man who betrays the Son of Man! It would be better for him if he had not been born."

THE PASSOVER

THE PASSOVER WAS A REMEMBRANCE OF ISRAEL'S EXODUS FROM EGYPT. COMMEMORATED WAS THE "PASSING OVER" OF GOD'S JUDGMENT, WHEN ALL JEWISH HOMES MARKED BY THE BLOOD OF A "PASSOVER" LAMB WERE SPARED FROM DEATH. THE LAST SUPPER TAKES PLACE AT THAT MOMENT IN ISRAEL WHEN ALL THE CELEBRATORY LAMBS WERE BEING SLAUGHTERED FOR THE PASSOVER FEASTS. THIS SETTING CLEARLY POINTS TO JESUS AS THE ULTIMATE PASSOVER SACRIFICE: "THE LAMB OF GOD WHO TAKES AWAY THE SINS OF THE WORLD" (JOHN 1:29).

1 Stereotypes and Labels

Survey Says

✳ "Even though we are told we can be whatever we want to be, there is still pressure to do and become the same old gender roles."

8th-grade girl

✳ "You feel very pressured to fit into the mold that makes up the tradition and most of us girls don't want to. I AM going to be a police officer whether people tell me to or not."

12th-grade girl

✳ 57 percent of girls said that parents want girls to play with dolls, not trucks and action figures.

✳ 55 percent of girls said it is true that girls are expected to speak softly and not cause trouble.

✳ 50 percent of girls said it is true that girls are expected to spend a lot of their time on housework and taking care of younger brothers and sisters.

✳ 38 percent of girls said that people think girls don't know how to take care of their own money.

✳ 17 percent of girls said that teachers think it is not important for girls to be good at math.

Get Beyond Pink and Blue

The next time you're shopping at your local department store, head over to the baby section for a quick little experiment. Imagine you are an explorer surveying the land. What's your take on this uncharted territory? Chances are, you'll find yourself looking at two separate continents: The Republic of Princesses (capital: Frillsville) and the United States of Sports (national pastimes: soccer, baseball, basketball, and football). One is pretty in pink and the other is tried-and-true blue. You might spot a few pastel-yellow and -green islands here and there, but they are easily swallowed up by the two dominating colors in this region. Of course there's certainly nothing wrong with pink. And blue is perfectly respectable, too. Here's the question: which color is meant for which gender? It's a no-brainer, isn't it? That's because we all get an early introduction to how girls and boys are treated differently in our world. Baby girls' cribs are lined with Darling Daisy–brand blankets, Enchanted Garden sheets, and NoJo Princess Dreams pillows. Over on that other continent, baby boys get bedding from the Animal Antics, Lil Bear Sport, or Batter's Up collection.

Now let's take this experiment a few steps further—to your local drugstore. Stroll down the greeting cards aisle and check out the kiddie cards. You'll find fairies, princesses, ponies, and kittens bringing birthday greetings like, "For a special girl who's one: a sweet girl who's huggable, snuggable, and loveable, too!" and "To extra special sweet and cuddly you!" The cards for boys are not quite so warm and fuzzy. There are baseballs, basketballs, dump trucks, and a motorcycle card that says, "Fire it Up, Little Man!" A boy on a skateboard has this birthday message: "Show 'em what you're made of! Blaze your birthday trail."

So what's the big deal? Shouldn't little girls be allowed to prance around in tutus and glittery plastic tiaras if that's what makes them happy? Absolutely. And what's so terrible about little boys having big dreams of slam dunks and grand slams? Not a thing! Gender stereotypes aren't really about princesses or pinch hitters, anyway. The pressures come from the messages girls and boys get about what they should look like, act like, and grow up to be like. And all those "shoulds" can make it hard to feel confident about the unique things that *do* make you amazing. What do you truly care about? Whom do you want to become? Whether your passion is world travel, fashion, biology, or baseball, the truth is that girls don't have to be "sweet and cuddly" to make a difference in the world. And boys don't always have to be "little men" and take charge of everything all the time. Girls and boys should have equal opportunities to pursue their interests and reach their goals, whatever they might be.

Did You Know?

In 1972, Title IX made a big splash. What is Title IX exactly? A summer blockbuster sequel? Nope. An over-the-counter, immune-boosting super vitamin? Guess again. Title IX is a federal law that says sex discrimination in schools is a big no-no. *Legally, that means girls and boys should be given equal opportunities to participate in all educational programs, including sports.* Almost 3 million girls play school sports today—that's ten times the number of girls who played before Title IX went into effect! However, many schools still give girls the short end of the stick when it comes to funding for athletics programs. Too often, girls' teams have to settle for second-rate equipment and facilities while the boys at their schools are fully decked out and hooked up.

Girl goes to college. Girl graduates with a bachelor's degree and scores a great new job. Girl gets her first paycheck. Guy goes to college, graduates with a bachelor's degree, and nabs a similar position. Guy gets his first paycheck. *These two have the same credentials—so why aren't they making the same salary?* According to a recent study conducted by the American Association of University Women, guys who are one year out of college are already earning 20 percent more than their female counterparts. Talk about an unfair wage gap!

Lawrence Summers was the president of Harvard University in 2005, when he made some public remarks implying that *women do not have the same innate abilities as men in the areas of math, science, and engineering.* That statement did not go over well with the women scientists who happened to be in the audience.

Nancy Hopkins, who has a Ph.D. in molecular biology, was so angry that she packed up her laptop and walked out on his speech.

In fact, girls and women have the same abilities as boys and men when it comes to math and science. "There are all of these myths about why women don't go into science. They do go into science," former U.S. Secretary of Health and Human Services Donna Shalala told The Harvard Crimson. "Women take the classes but don't get hired as professors." Hmmm, now there's an idea for Summers. Maybe instead of talking about women scientists, he should have been hiring them!

Try This: Read the Labels

Match these girls and guys to their labels.

Labels

1. Matt, 15 He made the varsity basketball team in his freshman year. Everyone in school is talking about going all the way to state championships this year—and Matt's the one who will lead the team to victory. He always makes his presence known and can be heard shouting "Dude!" to his boys in the hallways between classes.

a. "Emo"

2. Jessica, 12 She never travels anywhere without her compact. After lunch, you can find her in the bathroom curling her eyelashes and applying her tenth coat of lip gloss. She spends her weekends scoping out sales at the mall.

b. "Girly Girl"

3. Dwayne, 13 He sports vintage T-shirts, skinny boy jeans, and wire-rimmed glasses (although it's hard to get a glimpse of them through his overgrown bangs). Never without his sketch pad and iPod, he keeps to himself and doesn't smile much.

c. "Tomboy"

4. Veronica, 15 Her idea of fashion is sweatpants and her worn-in, grease-stained hoodie. Forget fixing hair; this girl loves to fix cars! She works part time at the local body shop with her BFF, Mike. Everyone is curious about what she'll wear to prom. No one has ever seen her in a skirt!

d. "Jock"

How did you do?
Answers: 1-d, 2-b, 3-a, 4-c
OK, so that was a breeze. See how you do with these:

1. Shannon, 11 She spent a year in Japan when her father was relocated there for business. Even though the move was hard at first, she grew to appreciate the opportunity to experience a totally new culture (sushi is now her fave). Shannon is considering studying international business when she goes to college.

a. "Party Animal"

2. Justin, 12 He became a local celebrity at the age of 10, when he rescued his 3-year-old neighbor from a swimming pool. After school, he can be found at the local movie theater. An aspiring filmmaker, he sees every new movie in its opening week.

b. "Diva"

3. Dominique, 15 She learned sign language to communicate with her cousin, who is deaf. She signs every week for the Sunday service at her church, and she plays drums in a band that has opened for some big indie-rock headliners.

c. "Math Geek"

4. Gerald, 14 After graduation, this future top chef is heading straight for culinary school. He's got a serious sweet tooth, and has been testing out recipes for what he hopes will be deemed The Best Brownies on Earth (Ever!).

d. "Flirt"

Hmmm, did you figure it out? Dominique might be the Math Geek, but she could also be the Flirt, the Diva, or even the Party Animal! Actually, none of those labels points to any of the facts you learned about Dominique, Gerald, Justin, or Shannon. Food labels reveal what's inside that bag of chips or can of soup, but people labels don't work the same way. In fact, when you label people, you might be missing out on some of their most important qualities. Stereotypes and labels are damaging, and unfortunately they are everywhere—at home, at school, and in the working world, too. The good news is that the more we are able to recognize them, the better prepared we will be to stand up to them and make changes.

✏ Journal It!

Fill in the blank:

Girls are supposed to

_____

_____

_____

Boys are supposed to

_____

_____

_____

Girls are not supposed to

_____

_____

_____

Boys are not supposed to

_____

_____

_____

Do you think these expectations are fair? Think of a time when you experienced a gender stereotype or label. How did you handle it?

"A couple of my friends who are boys came to school today wearing girls' socks (like pink with rainbows and stuff) and one of our teachers said they were ridiculous and to roll their pants down. He was implying that they looked like girls and that made me angry. Kids should be able to dress how they want."

Shelby, 12

"I love to sing folk songs, play soccer, run cross country, and many other things. There are guidelines that all girls feel they have to follow. Like all women have to have large breasts and be under 120 pounds. I am constantly teased on how I dress and how I love to run and get hot and sweaty. Many girls look at me with distaste and hatred as I run and get muddy with the boys. If I could change something about growing up as a girl, it would be to banish all stereotypes. But I feel that it is good that people like me are willing to step out of the boundaries."

Guanshan, 14

Advice from Amazing Girls

Do Your Best and Play Your Hardest

Cryshawna, 18, takes no prisoners when it comes to playing Ping-Pong. But her stellar skills became the subject of sexist comments when a male staff member at the community center where she attends Girls Inc. programs found out that she had just won a game against a boy. He teased the boy for losing a "male-dominated" game. Cryshawna thinks his attitude needs some big-time adjustment. "I don't understand how you can have 'male-dominated' games," she says. As far as she's concerned, she dominated that game.

Don't Let Anyone Dismiss Your Problems

Madrianne, 18, has noticed that stereotypes sometimes make it harder for girls to be taken seriously when they're having conflicts with one another. "Why are girls always called 'catty' when we argue with each other?" she asks. "Boys aren't the only ones who have 'real' fights. 'Catfight' implies that girls' issues aren't serious."

Follow Your Own Path

Arlene, 17, has been thinking about becoming a crime scene investigator, an idea her dad was not too happy to hear about. "He is encouraging me to be a secretary because it's 'safer,'" she says. Arlene gets where her dad is coming from, but she can't help but wonder if he would be freaking out so much if she were a guy. Arlene is determined to keep her options open and continue exploring the possibility of a career in forensic science, so she participated in a Girls Inc. summer program called Eureka! that gave her hands-on experience in science, math, and technology.

Don't Make Assumptions

Selina, 17, is smart, stylish, and well-spoken. She says that people often make false assumptions about girls based on stereotypes: "People think that if you look like a tomboy, you're automatically comfortable with yourself and if you look like you stepped out of *Vogue*, you're trying to impress everyone." She says you can never know a girl's true personality and interests just by sizing up her style.

Selina's favorite program at Girls Inc. is Botball. She works with a team of girls to build robots that compete in a tournament. This future math major is all too aware of how gender stereotypes can limit girls' abilities to take risks and try new activities. Last year, her Botball team was the only all-girls team to compete in the state tournament.

Role Model Remedy: First Impressions Can Be Deceiving

After more than thirty years of working in major corporations, Jean Otte founded her own company called WOMEN (Women's Organization for Mentoring, Education and Networking) Unlimited,

Inc. WOMEN Unlimited is a nationwide organization focused on cultivating leadership excellence. In other words, it's Jean's job to help women be the best leaders they can be in their careers. She had a lot of leadership experience behind her, but she says it was her experience working with diverse groups of people that helped the most when she was launching her company. Her biggest cheerleader was her former boss Jack Yurish. When Jean and Jack first met, she feared that he was just another guy in a business suit, and he wondered if she would be too "emotional" to deal with. The two were complete opposites, or so it seemed. Jean is bubbly, outgoing, and funny. Jack is reserved, quiet, and serious. OK, so technically Jack *is* a guy who wears a business suit, and it's true that Jean has no problem speaking with lots of energy and enthusiasm. But these two didn't let first impressions or stereotypes cloud their judgment. And they didn't try to change each other or themselves. By working together and really getting to know each other, Jean and Jack discovered that their different styles were a very good match—and they always got the job done. Today, Jean gives Jack a lot of credit for giving her the confidence to make her biggest and best career decisions, including starting WOMEN Unlimited!

Try This: Spot the Media Stereotypes

The characters you see in the media don't always represent how people look and act in real life. TV, movies, magazines, video games, and the Internet sometimes use stereotypes to make a quick point or to make an audience laugh. For instance, have you ever seen a boy-crazy, fashion-obsessed teen girl character in a movie or on a sitcom? What about a scatter-brained scientist? Of course not all girls' lives revolve around boys and shopping, and not all scientists are so wacky and out there, but you probably wouldn't know that if you were getting all your information straight from the media. The problem with stereotypes is that they offer a very limited picture of all the different kinds of people in the world.

Take one week to record the stereotypes you see on your TV, computer and any movies you see, as well as the characters who are breaking stereotypes. Use this checklist as you go.

Check any of these stereotypes you see, and add any other you find:

✔ Stereotypes

- ○ An overweight person eating junk food
- ○ A teen or tween girl obsessed with her looks or with boys
- ○ A goofy boy falling down or making a fool of himself while trying to impress a girl
- ○ A wife nagging her husband to do a chore
- ○ A husband watching sports on TV while his wife cooks or cleans
- ○ Other: _____
- ○ Other: _____
- ○ Other: _____

Now, check any of these "un-stereotypes" you see, and add any others you find:

✔ Breaking Stereotypes

- ○ A girl who is strong, smart, and bold
- ○ A boy who is sensitive and caring
- ○ A husband and wife who share the housework equally
- ○ An older person who is able to take care of himself or herself
- ○ Other: _____
- ○ Other: _____
- ○ Other: _____

✎ Journal It!

Were any of the stereotypes you saw harmful?

_____

_____

_____

How could you re-write those scenes without using stereotypes?

_____

_____

_____

✉ Instant Messages

To: Teachers, parents, adults in my life

From: AmazingGirl101

How were the stereotypes about girls and boys different when you were growing up? Are there some stereotypes that still exist? Write me back.

Send!

To: My representatives, legislators, and school board

From: AmazingGirl101

As a girl growing up today, it's important to me that girls and boys have equal opportunities for success in academics, sports, and careers. Here are some things I would like to change about the gender stereotypes at my school and in my community:

_____

Send!

To: TV and movie executives

From: AmazingGirl101

I want to see lots of different girl and boy characters with lots of different experiences and opinions . . . not just princesses and action heroes! The shows and movies I think have good characters for girls are:

_____

_____

_____

The shows that have the same old stereotypes are:

_____

_____

_____

Send!

2 | Looks

Survey Says

✳ "Even today, society values beauty in girls over intelligence."

9th-grade girl

✳ "I feel that we are expected to be grown up now. We are supposed to dress like older girls."

6th-grade girl

✳ 84 percent of girls said that girls are under a lot of pressure to dress the right way.

✳ 74 percent of girls said that the most popular girls in school are thin.

✳ 69 percent of girls worry about their appearance.

✳ 52 percent of girls worry about their weight.

If you're familiar with the show *America's Next Top Model*, you know that each episode ends with the contestants standing before a panel of judges, who critique them on their style, makeup techniques, facial expressions, body language, and pretty much everything in between. Although most girls don't have supermodels, stylists, or "noted fashion photographers" picking their looks apart on a daily basis, there's plenty of beauty pressure in the real world, too. From choosing the right outfit to worrying about your skin and hair to freaking out about your body size or having the right clothing brands, sometimes it can seem as if you're preparing to appear before a panel of your very own judges every day—even if you're just getting ready to go to school or out to the movies.

On the bright side, your real life isn't reality TV. In fact, you call the shots on your show! The great thing about being an amazing girl is that you never have to stand silently waiting for some dramatic, tearful elimination; you can start speaking your mind and defining what beauty means to *you*! The first step is recognizing the "judges" and pressures in your life so you can learn how to deal with them—and how to do it with strong, smart, and bold style!

Try This: Rate the Judges!

This section covers three kinds of "judges" who can make girls feel insecure about their looks. How would you rate each?

1. Serious pressure cooker! This one always makes me feel like I don't measure up.
2. Medium heat, but not quite boiling. This one sometimes makes me feel "unpretty."
3. Easy, breezy, no pressure! This one never makes me feel bad about my looks.

The Media

In today's world, you can barely make a move without seeing an image of some "perfect" model or celebrity. Magazines, TV, movies, music videos, advertisements, and Web sites are everywhere, and they all have plenty of messages about what beautiful people are supposed to look like and act like. The problem is that what we see in the media doesn't always match up too well with reality. Your rating: _____

> "Beer commercials show that guys are only interested in women that are gorgeous and skinny. It makes one think that I must look like that to be accepted or loved."
>
> *Meghan, 16*

Friends and Peers

Most girls want to fit in, and that wish for acceptance can go hand-in-hand with the wish to have the "right" look. There are trends to follow, brands on the must-have list, and the ever-present reminder that certain body types seem to get more attention. There's also the sad but true reality that teasing happens, and it's not much fun to be on the receiving end. Your rating: _____

> "A lot of the girls at my school are really skinny and they're the most popular girls. I'm glad I'm not that skinny, but I feel jealous a lot of the time because they're so popular and well-liked."
>
> *Melinda, 14*

Parents, Family, and Teachers

Adults in your life say they want what's best for you, but that doesn't necessarily mean that you will agree on what "best for you" really means. Whether they're imposing rules and restrictions about what you can and can't wear or dropping not-so-subtle comments about your weight or your changing body, it sometimes feels like adults just don't get it. And to top it off, adults (especially women) face their own share of beauty and body insecurities, so some girls go from hearing about their friends' diets at school to hearing about their moms' diets at home. Your rating: _____

"A friend of mine wasn't allowed to wear makeup at the beginning of the year and everyone else was wearing makeup. So she got us to put makeup on her at lunch and then she'd wipe it off before she went home, just to be like us, and because she didn't feel good enough about herself. She got caught and her mom was mad but said that because she was going to do it anyway, that she could wear it."

Nadine, 13

Role Model Remedy: Runway Reality Check!

Magali Amadei has appeared on the pages and covers of *Glamour, Vogue, Cosmopolitan, Elle,* and *Marie Claire,* but her top-model status didn't make Magali feel good about herself—it actually made her feel worse. Magali suffered with depression and bulimia through the height of her modeling career. "Sure, the pictures of me are pretty, but that was all a fantasy," Magali says. "It had nothing to do with how I was feeling in my real life."

Today, Magali travels around the country to talk to girls about her experiences in the fashion and beauty industry. "Lots of girls tell me they want to be models, and I'm not surprised," she says. "On the surface, it looks like a pretty fabulous job. But if you think that being a model will make you feel better about yourself, you are in for a huge disappointment. The modeling world is the last place I would recommend for a girl with insecurities. There is so much rejection and you're constantly judged on your appearance." Fashion and beauty can be fun, but Magali's experience has taught her that physical beauty is never the ticket to happiness or confidence. As for all those glossy, perfect images? Magali uses real examples from her own modeling career to show girls how nearly all the pictures we see in magazines are altered. "It's not just erasing a pimple here and there. They can change a model's entire face and body. My teeth have been straightened, my waist has been thinned, and I even got 'digital breast implants' for the cover of *Cosmopolitan.* Believe me, there is no beauty product in existence that works as well as Photoshop!"

Role Model Remedy: Red Carpet Reality Check!

As a professional photographer, Duffy-Marie Arnoult is often hired to cover red carpet events. Her portfolio includes pictures of some of the world's most famous faces, including Justin Timberlake, Mary J. Blige, Lance Armstrong, and even Hillary Clinton! There is plenty of glitz and glamour that comes with photographing celebrities, but at the end of the day Duffy-Marie knows how important it is to take a step back from all A-list craziness. "I think magazines encourage a little too much interest in celebrity lives," she says. "We don't need to know everything that is going on with them. We need to take time to focus on our lives and our future goals. It is easy to get distracted with Hollywood."

If you think you feel pressure to have the right look, Duffy-Marie says Hollywood can feel like the world's largest popularity contest, where everyone is watching the stars and talking about them behind their backs. "It can be especially difficult for women celebrities, since they are expected to be picture-perfect twenty-four hours a day and be walking fashion advertisements," she says. "This is a lot of pressure, especially when there seems to be a desire to see these women when they aren't so glamorous. Certain photographers will do anything to get a shot of them like this." Duffy-Marie is definitely *not* one of those photographers. In fact, she has a policy that she will not take a picture of anyone who doesn't want to be photographed, and if she somehow ends up with an unflattering photo of a celebrity that could be used for bad publicity, she won't release it.

Duffy-Marie thinks it's fine for girls to enjoy a little celebrity media here and there, as long as it doesn't keep you from working toward your real-life goals and dreams. "I look at the celebrity element as only part of what I do," she says. "It can be fun and exciting, but I am more interested in taking photos of people you might not know about and telling their story." Duffy says one of her favorite projects took place thousands of miles from the Hollywood red carpet: "I took some photos of a soccer game in the remote coastal fishing village of Andavadoaka, Madagascar (an island off the southeastern coast of

Africa). The ocean was in the background, and the villagers sat on the rocks while the teams competed. It was surreal."

Beauty Buzzword Scavenger Hunt

What words make us dip into our wallets? Advertisers know them. Can you find them? The next time you're flipping through a magazine, pick up a pen. Search for these beauty buzzwords, and circle them. For an extra challenge, do this activity with a group of friends. See who can find the most words in her magazine!

Miracle, Perfect, Radiant, Dream, Beautiful, Natural, Inspiration, New, Sugar-free, Low-fat, Low-calorie, Proven, Clinically proven, Hydrating, Pore, Volume, Fullness, Moisture/Moisturizing, Shine, Breakthrough, Healthy

Journal It!

Why do you think beauty buzzwords appear so often in beauty advertisements? What do these words have in common?

_____

_____

_____

Think of a time when you wanted to buy a product based on the ad. Was there a buzzword or an image that caught your eye?

_____

_____

_____

If you created an advertisement, what would it look like? What would it say?

_____

_____

_____

Try This: Make Your Amazing Beauty Playlist

Imagine your perfect music mix. It could be a party playlist to get you and your friends dancing. Or maybe it's for your ears only—a collection of special tunes that make your heart sing. Creating a mix is all about choosing a balance of different artists, beats, and harmonies. Each of these elements adds up to one incredible music experience that has you written all over it!

Beauty is also a uniquely personal mix. It's about what's on the outside (your style and your "look") and what's on the inside (the amazing traits that make you glow). To feel truly beautiful, we all have to find a balance between inner beauty and outer beauty. It can be easy to get caught up in thinking about your clothes, your hair, or your weight, but let's face it: your playlist will be pretty boring if it's all about your physical appearance. Would you want to listen to the same song on repeat all day, every day? We didn't think so!

Instructions:

Amazing Beauty Playlist has six slots. First, choose your top three inner-beauty and outer-beauty traits.

My top three inner-beauty traits:
(Examples: "I'm a good friend," "I'm smart," "I have a good sense of humor")

1. _____

2. _____

3. _____

My top three outer-beauty traits:
(Examples: "I have a nice smile," "I have great accessories," "I have pretty eyes")

1. _____

2. _____

3. _____

Now it's time to mix up your beauty traits in the order that creates just the right balance for you! How will you kick things off, and what will you pick for your best finish?

My Amazing Beauty Playlist

1. _____

2. _____

3. _____

4. _____

5. _____

6. _____

Role Model Remedy: Make Peace With Your Body

Ann Shoket is the editor-in-chief of *Seventeen*. Her magazine reaches millions of teens, but she believes that girls and women of all ages should embrace positive attitudes about beauty and body image. Ann has heard lots of "love your body" buzz in the ten years she's worked in publishing. Meanwhile, the pressures girls deal with have only gotten more intense.

"When you tell a girl to 'love her body,' she's going to say, 'Yeah, right,'" Ann explains. So this editor is taking a different approach to helping girls appreciate who they are on the inside and on the outside. It's called the *Seventeen* Body Peace Project. "I'm not asking you to always love your body. I'm just asking you to make peace with it," she says.

As part of this project, Ann is inviting every girl to sign the Body Peace Treaty, a promise to stop obsessing over size and start treating your body with respect. In just two months, the treaty was signed by 16,000 girls! Among the first to add their names were celebrities including Ciara, Pink, Carrie Underwood, Miley Cyrus, and Kelly Osbourne. The thirteen international editions of *Seventeen* magazine also feature the Body Peace Project, which means that girls all around the globe will get to sign the treaty, too.

At the heart of the Body Peace Project is the message to accept yourself and support other girls. "Girls are bashing themselves, and that's damaging," Ann warns. You might think you're helping a friend by reassuring her that she looks great when she says she feels fat. But really you're just getting stuck in a conversation that's going nowhere. Ann's advice is to change the subject and talk about talents instead of appearances: "Give your friend props for something she's good at. Don't focus on what she looks like."

The Seventeen Body Peace Treaty

I vow to . . .

* Remember that the sun will still rise tomorrow even if I had one too many slices of pizza or an extra scoop of ice cream tonight.

* Never blame my body for the bad day I'm having.

* Stop joining in when my friends compare and trash their own bodies.

* Never allow a dirty look from someone else to influence how I feel about my appearance.

* Quit judging a person solely by how his or her body looks—even if it seems harmless—because I'd never want anyone to do that to me.

* Notice all the amazing things my body is doing for me every moment I walk, talk, think, breathe . . .

* Quiet that negative little voice in my head when it starts to say mean things about my body that I'd never tolerate anyone else saying about me.

* Remind myself that what you see isn't always what you get on TV and in ads—it takes a lot of

airbrushing, dieting, money, and work to look like that.

✳ Remember that even the girl who I'd swap bodies with in a minute has something about her looks that she hates.

✳ Respect my body by feeding it well, working up a sweat when it needs it, and knowing when to give it a break.

✳ Realize that the mirror can reflect only what's on the surface of me, not who I am inside.

✳ Know that I'm already beautiful just the way I am.

Signed,

Advice from Amazing Girls

Stand Up to Adults

As a HEART (Helping Everyone Achieve Respect Together) peer counselor, Madrianne, 18, once worked with a student who came to her because her cross-country coach was pressuring her to lose weight. "The coach wanted her to go on the Atkins diet so she could run faster," Madrianne remembers. "It was a real dilemma for her because the coach was an authority figure and being on the team was a really big deal—it required a lot of sacrifice and dedication." In the end, the girl decided that this kind of diet was an unhealthy sacrifice she was unwilling to make. She needed to be strong and well-nourished in order to truly dedicate herself to the team. With Madrianne's support, she explained her feelings to the coach, and he backed off.

Stand Up for Other Girls

Christine, 12, is fed up with mean girls who make fun of other girls for what they're wearing. "I feel there's a lot of pressure from other girls, which I think is the worst because we should be sticking together, right?" she says. If Christine sees a girl getting teased, she doesn't just sit on the sidelines. "Girls at my school will insult you or hint that they don't like your outfit," she says. "Whenever I see them doing that to another girl, I try to stand up for her and compliment her because they can be really harsh!"

What's Your "True to You" Style?

Style and fashion are fun ways to express what's unique about you! Style is not about squeezing your body into a certain cut of jeans just because that's what other girls are wearing. It's not about having the most expensive brands or wearing the most makeup, either. Girls with real style know how to show up with confidence because they know what they like and what looks good on them. Fill in the blanks to help discover your very own "true to you" style!

My favorite colors are _____ .

The outfit I feel most comfortable and confident in is _____
_____ because
_____ .

When I think of the word stylish I think of _____ .

The item in my wardrobe that is uniquely me is _____
_____ .

The inner beauty qualities I would like to shine through in my style are _____ .

Take this list with you on your next shopping trip for inspiration!

To: My friends

From: AmazingGirl101

Here's something I just learned about my style: (insert an item from your "true to you" style list here, for example). Your turn! How would you have answered that one? Write me back.

Send!

To: Magazine editors

From: AmazingGirl101

The things in your magazine that make me feel good about my looks are:

The things that make me feel bad about my looks are:

I would like to see these changes:

Send!

To: A female adult you trust (you choose the person, or send to a few people!)

From: AmazingGirl101

How did you look when you were my age? How did you feel about your looks? What was your image of the "perfect" body? How has it changed? Let's talk!

Send!

3 School

Survey Says

✳ "It is not fair that girls are expected to behave better at school than boys."

6th-grade girl

✳ "It is hard. You have to be pretty and have a body to be popular and if you are too smart you are called a nerd. But, you have to be extra smart to even get a job after college."

5th-grade girl

✳ 71 percent of girls aspire to go to college after high school graduation.

✳ 65 percent of girls said that they worry about getting good grades in school.

✳ 62 percent of girls said that they feel stressed about having too much homework.

✳ 56 percent of girls said that they feel stressed about having too many tests at school.

✳ 55 percent of girls said that they feel stressed about not being able to do everything their teachers want them to do.

✳ 55 percent of girls said that in their schools, boys think they have the right to comment on girls' bodies.

✳ 44 percent of girls said that the smartest girls in their school are not popular.

* 36 percent of girls said that it is true that people think girls are not interested in computers and technology.

* 17 percent of girls said that teachers think it is not as important for girls to be good at math.

How would you describe your school? Whatever words you choose, you're probably thinking of something a bit more detailed than "a building filled with classrooms," right? After all, you spend a big chunk of your time at school. You learn a lot about yourself during those hours—much more than you could ever learn just from reading textbooks or studying for tests. School is where you form important friendships and bond with teachers. It's also a place where you can discover your talents and let them shine! On the flip side, there are sure to be classes and activities that don't come as naturally to you, along with uncomfortable situations and teachers and peers who are pretty far down on your "people I would take with me to a desert island" list. Some mornings you might want to hide under the covers when that alarm blares in your ear. Other days might seem too short because you're having so much fun. And sometimes a hide-under-the-covers morning will turn itself around and become one of those I-can't-believe-this-day-is-over-already afternoons. The point is that school can be a bumpy roller coaster, but all those bumps don't have to derail you.

There are more educational opportunities for girls than ever before, which is good news. Unfortunately, all those opportunities can add up to a lot more pressure. Nowadays, girls don't just talk about what they want to be when they grow up; they worry about what college they will go to, how they'll get in, and how they will pay for it. That good old A for effort doesn't always feel like it's worth as much if there's no A to match it on the report card.

There's no doubt about it: school is a push and pull. You're working hard to be a standout student, athlete, writer, artist, actor, and all around supergirl at the head of your class. Meanwhile, you're also trying to fit in, look pretty, and just feel normal when you're walking down the halls. Is it possible to perform this balancing act without toppling over under the weight of your parents', teachers', and friends' expectations? Good question!

Try This: Make the Grade

When you work hard for a good grade, you deserve to feel proud of yourself when you get it. But sometimes when you put too much focus on getting the end result you want, you can miss out on some great lessons in the process. These girls all took the same test on women's voting rights, and they all got different grades. Here's the twist: grade them again based on what they really learned, not just on the facts they memorized. Will they get high marks? You make the call!

Janie made flash cards to help her remember all the names and dates on her "Women's Voting Rights Timeline." She can match "1920" to "the year the Nineteenth Amendment was signed into law, granting women the right to vote," and she knows that the Seneca Falls Convention took place in 1848. She got both of those answers right on the test, even though she's not sure what actually happened at the Seneca Falls Convention. Her teacher didn't spend much time discussing it in class, so Janie figured it wasn't worth knowing since it probably wasn't going to be on the test.

✳ What did Janie learn? _____

✳ Janie's test grade: A

✳ How would you grade Janie's learning experience?

_____

As soon as she saw the "Women's Suffrage Movement" chapter headline in her textbook, Tricia remembered the funny "Sister Suffragette" song from *Mary Poppins*. She raised her hand and asked her teacher if the song was related to what they were learning. Not only did her teacher say that it was related, but she brought in the *Mary Poppins* DVD the next day so that the whole class could watch that part of the movie and discuss the song's lyrics! Everyone was cracking up at how cheesy it was, but most of the kids did admit that they'd had no idea what that song was about. Plus everyone was excited to have a little comic relief in the classroom!

* What did Tricia learn? _____
* Tricia's test grade: C+
* How would you grade Tricia's learning experience?

_____

As secretary of the student council, Patti was especially interested in learning about how women got the right to vote and how they exercise their rights today. While she was studying for the test, she also started working on an article for the school newspaper. She incorporated facts from the textbook and handouts, along with her opinions about why girls and boys should care about the political process. A few older students even congratulated her at lunch on the day the article was published!

* What did Patti learn? _____
* Patti's test grade: B
* How would you grade Patti's learning experience?

_____

Most girls strive for good grades, but sometimes the grade you see on the test or the report card doesn't reflect everything you've learned. The next time you get a grade, think about how you would grade your learning experience. Talk about that with your parents and your teacher, too. Even though your actual grade might not always be an A+, what can you do in the future to make sure your learning-experience grade is?

Advice from Amazing Girls

You Don't Have to Be in a Classroom to Learn Something Cool (and Useful!) at School

Jordan, 12, was challenged to an offbeat learning opportunity when she was least expecting it. "One day at recess my teacher found me and my friend sitting in the grass. I was drawing on my friend's arm with a Sharpie (my friend asked me to) and I was worried my teacher would get mad, but she didn't! She told me that she thought I was a very good artist but she didn't know if permanent marker on skin was very healthy. She asked me to do a bit of research on that topic, so I did! I gave her a two page report on the effects of Sharpie on skin. The results were inconclusive, but I feel like I learned a lot about it! And it was actually really interesting!"

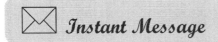

Instant Message

To: A friend or peer at school

From: AmazingGirl101

The most interesting thing I've learned at school (remember, it can be something either in a classroom or outside a classroom!) this year is _____
_____. What about you? Write me back!

Send!

Amazing Teachers

Every teacher has a different style. Some are strict and some are relaxed. Some are funny and entertaining, while others might make you want to put your head down on the desk and take a nice long nap. School yearbooks give students awards like "most likely to succeed" and "best dressed," but how would you award your teachers? Think about whom you would give these titles to and why.

Best listener

_____

Awarded because

_____

Most likely to moonlight as a standup comedian

_____

Awarded because

_____

Most fair

_____

Awarded because

_____

Most creative

_____

Awarded because

_____

Most likely to give me a good pep talk

_____

Awarded because

_____

Most likely to encourage me to try something new

_____

Awarded because

_____

> "The teacher who taught my Science class was so cool! We could ask her anything, totally off subject, and she'd answer. She knew stories about anything, and she kept us updated with new discoveries in science."

Caroline, 13

> "My favorite teacher taught us life skills, which in my opinion is more important than any other subject taught in school! She was also very kind and caring, and I felt comfortable around her."

Erin, 12

> "My favorite teacher let us talk about things and didn't judge. When there were problems at the school, she wouldn't try to hide it from us like the other teachers did. This teacher never spoke to us in a condescending way."

Ellie, 15

Try This: Draw a Map of Your School

From *The Supergirl Dilemma*: "Just today a boy had a very revealing image of a young girl and the teacher didn't do a thing about it when she saw it either. . . . What girls need is to be able to trust adults to talk about what they're facing."

8th-grade girl

The Girls Inc. Girls' Bill of Rights states that "a girl has a right to have confidence in herself and be safe in the world." Do you feel confident and safe at school? Get out a piece of paper and draw a map of your school. Circle any spots where you or other girls might feel unsure of yourself or threatened. How do you deal with those spaces?

Send an instant message to an adult you trust to share your map and talk about what changes need to be made to make the school safe for all girls.

✉ Instant Message

To: A teacher or other adult I trust

From: AmazingGirl101

I made a map that shows where girls might feel unsafe or unsure of themselves at my school. Girls deserve to feel safe and confident. I would like to make an appointment to discuss my map with you. Write me back!

Send!

Role Model Remedy: Focus on the 'Doing' and Not on the 'Achieving'

How does a girl voted "most quiet" in the seventh grade grow up to become a TV news reporter? Just ask SuChin Pak. She has been in front of the MTV cameras for years, but SuChin clearly recalls her middle school days. Back then, she was a shy girl whose biggest fear was being left to fend for herself in the chaotic shuffle in the hallways.

"I had this one friend with blonde hair and blue eyes. She was outgoing, popular, and didn't care what anyone thought of her—basically everything I wasn't. But she was nice to me, so I would literally just cling to her. The bell would ring and I would hold onto her backpack, tagging behind her from class to class like she was my lifeline. I was so terrified of being out there on my own," she says.

In high school, a teacher encouraged SuChin to join the debate team, and she decided to take the risk and try it. "That was the first time I started to see myself as something other than the quiet Korean immigrant. I had found something I was good at!" she remembers. "The confidence I gained from debating filtered into other parts of my life, too. I started to really believe that I was more than just the jeans I was wearing or how skinny or pretty I was."

SuChin also has learned that overcoming your fears and building on your strengths is a lifelong process. "You can set goals and meet them—that's great. But there's never this big peak of the mountain that defines you as an official 'success.' When I got hired at MTV, I thought, 'Now this is it.' I had made it big. I had this idea that I would start turning up on the cover of *Vogue* or something," she says. "But here I am years later, doing my job and enjoying my experiences. Don't forget that your real life is in the 'doing,' not in the achievements, magazine covers, trophies, or grades."

Try This: Your Locker Portrait

Have you decorated the inside of your locker? The pressures of the school day can be draining, so think of your locker as the place where you can refuel between classes and remind yourself of what makes you an amazing girl! Some girls personalize their lockers with pictures or mirrors. Make this locker portrait, and you'll have a little of both!

* Draw a simple outline of a girl on a large piece of plain white paper.

* At the top of her head, write, "What do I think about/dream about?"

* On the right hand, write, "What do I spend my money on?"

* On the left hand, write, "How do I spend my time?"

* At the place over the heart, write, "What do I care about?"

* At the place over the belly, write, "What do I worry about?"

✳   At the base of the portrait, where the feet are, write, "What do I stand for/believe in?"

You can write in your answers, and you also can use personal photos, pictures from magazines, glitter, stickers, crayons, markers, or paint to represent your answers in a unique, colorful collage! Hang your portrait in your locker and look at it every day.

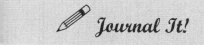

Journal It!

How would your locker portrait have looked if you had made it exactly one year ago?

_____

What things would be different?

_____

What things would be the same?

_____

What has changed in your life?

_____

Role Model Remedy: Geeks and Nerds Are Headed for Success

Julie Townsend builds robots and spaceships for a living! She was in charge of the NASA team responsible for sending commands to the Mars rovers, robots that explored the planet Mars and sent their findings back to Earth. Julie has been fascinated with robots and space exploration for as long as she can remember, and she is proud to say that her job is a dream come true. Julie worked hard to get where she is, and that meant embracing the fact that she might not always fit in. She knew that the skills and talents some kids made fun of were actually her ticket to an amazing career! "I got all sorts of trouble from the other kids about what a geek I was," she says. "In fact, I was never one of the popular girls, and I eventually just came to terms with that and decided it wasn't such a bad thing. I had plenty of other friends, and I got along just fine with all the other kids in my school, but they all thought I was a little bit strange because I was the only girl taking some of the advanced science courses." Out of the 16 students in her high school AP (advanced placement) physics class, Julie was the only girl. It was tough to feel that she was always trying to break through a stereotype, but she also knew what she needed to learn in order to get where she wanted to go. "There are some things that are just bigger than whether or not you're a geek," she tells girls. "You get out of middle school and high school, and even though they might have been a little harder for you since you weren't doing exactly what all the other mainstream kids were doing, it's the people who were the geeks, who didn't quite fit in, those are the people who are going to end up doing what they want to do in life."

4 Friends

Survey Says

✳ "[There is] lots of pressure to fit in when I just want to be myself."

   7th-grade girl

✳ 64 percent of girls in grades six through eight worry about fitting in.

✳ 58 percent of girls in grades six through eight worry about being teased or made fun of.

✳ 36 percent of girls in grades six through eight worry about whether others think they are cool.

Girls' Communities

In 1864, Girls Inc. was founded on the belief that amazing things happen when girls get together to be themselves. A lot has changed in the world since then, but our commitment to girls' communities is still going strong!

If you were to create your own community of supportive girls, who would you include? You probably thought of your closest friends first, didn't you? These are the girls who know how to make you laugh, who listen to you talk for hours about your crushes, and who let you vent on those days you wish you could just do over. You have your own language with your friends. Whether it's a hug, a cheer from the sidelines, or an "I'm so over this" eye roll, your friends make it clear that they get you and they're there for you.

Just as you could easily imagine who you would want to include in your supportive community, it's probably not too tough to think of a few girls who aren't all that supportive. Let's face it: being a girl is not always about giggly fun sleepovers and LOL moments. Some girls can be mean. You don't always know why they act the way they do, but there's no denying that it hurts to be teased, taunted, or left out—and these girls seem to be experts at all of those activities.

Then there are the girls who didn't immediately come to mind when you thought of creating your community. They don't have BFF status, but they're not mean girls, either. You see them at school, and you might share some classes with them. You don't know much about their interests, but they might have some valuable things to offer your community. What would happen if you decided to dig a little deeper?

Growing up means going through changes. In fact, pretty much everything in your life is changing! You transition from elementary school to middle school and then high school, you develop new interests and opinions, you feel the heat (and sometimes some heartbreak!) of crushes, your body starts developing, and your hormones start raging. Friendships can change, too. When friends you thought you knew suddenly start acting differently or hanging out with new kids, it can bring up a lot of feelings.

Girls' communities can help you deal with all the drama. Sure, you want your best friends there with you, but think about your community as an even bigger circle of girls. Every girl might not be experiencing *exactly* the same things you are, but we can guarantee that every girl is going through changes. How can you support other girls and how can you seek out their support? Being part of a strong community can reinforce your inner strength and your independence. Those are amazing skills you can use in every part of your life!

Advice from Amazing Girls

Opposites Attract

Stacey, 14, knows that she and her friend are very different, and although those differences come with challenges, they also have made their friendship more interesting. "My friend is Indonesian, dark skinned, 4'9" (and 15 years old), the youngest of three children, kind of moody, and from a *very* conservative and protective family. I'm European, olive-to-fair skinned, 5'10", the oldest of three children, very calm most of the time, and from a very free-thinking and non-constricting family.

"We look funny together, mainly because I'm a foot taller than she is, but I like to be around her because I like to hear from the perspective of a short person when I'm down on myself because I'm so tall (and I think it works the same way for her, too). However, our friendship can be challenging because I really disagree with her family's values. For example, she's a freshman in high school, and she's not allowed to spend a single night away from home!"

Journal It!

Which of your friends is least like you?

_____

What do you like about your differences?

_____

How do those differences make your friendship a challenge?

_____

Role Model Remedy: Does Your Friendship Need a Detox?

Sadie Gonzales, 21, is a former Girls Inc. scholar who is now an education major in college on her way to becoming a teacher. Looking back at her middle and high school years, Sadie sees that a lot of the friendships she tried to hold onto were actually not so good for her. "I call those friendships my 'toxic' friendships. I was always getting into fights with those girls. Sometimes I would want to do things like go to school dances. If they didn't want to go, I wouldn't go either. I was afraid of being alone, so I ended up hanging out with girls who lowered my self-esteem and held me back," she says.

A turning point for Sadie was when she tried out for a school play. "I auditioned with one of my friends. The idea was that we would do it together. But then I got cast as one of the seven dwarves (because I'm short!) and she got a different part, so we didn't really see each other that much during the rehearsals." That separation ended up being a blessing in disguise. "I had a fear of not being liked, which came from being rejected from cliques," Sadie recalls. "The best experience I had during that play was meeting new people and making new friends. We rocked as the seven dwarves!"

Advice from Amazing Girls

Make a 'No Interrupting' Rule

It can be stressful when you're stuck in the middle of a battle between friends. For Dolly, 13, the key to keeping the peace is listening. "I've had to resolve SOO many fights among friends. I get my friends to talk things through and make sure someone is around so they don't interrupt each other. If you hear what the other person says, problems are easier to fix."

Don't Put on a Fake Personality to Be Popular

Hannah, 12, says the best piece of advice she ever got from a friend was not to put on a fake personality, something she sees girls doing every day at her school. "Girls put on fake personalities sometimes so that they won't seem so different, so that they won't be excluded.

Because the girls who don't are often excluded from popular crowds," she says.

Journal It!

Have you ever had to resolve a conflict with a friend?

_____

How did you handle it?

_____

If you could go back and do it again, would you do anything differently?

_____

What was the best piece of advice a friend ever gave you?

_____

How did it help you in your life?

_____

What was the best piece of advice you gave to a friend?

_____

Try This: A-Maze-ing Communication

Successful friendships are built on good communication. How well do you communicate with your friends? Do this activity with a friend and find out!

finish

start

Choose which one of you will be the sender and which one will be the receiver. The receiver gets blindfolded and is handed a pencil. The sender can guide the receiver's hand to the maze, but after that, the sender must communicate verbally to help her trace her way through it. When the maze is completed, remove the blindfold and check out how you did! Which questions, words, or instructions were helpful, and which ones weren't? How would this activity apply to real life? Even though you might not be blindfolded, there are times when you might feel as if you are going blindly into a situation in which your friend has more information than you do. What can you take from this exercise that would help you during those times?

Advice from Amazing Girls

Say No to Mean Girl 2.0

When she attended Girls Inc. of Greater Houston, La'Sandra, 18, participated in a group project to raise awareness about online safety. "So many girls are on social networking websites like Facebook and MySpace. Those sites can be fun, but a lot of girls lie about their age and put information online that can be really dangerous," she says. La'Sandra also is aware that just as gossip and teasing is happening in schools, it's happening online, too. She remembers one girl in her town who was the victim of a nasty rumor that was started online. "Kids were saying that her mom was a prostitute and it got really ugly," she says. "I felt bad for that girl." To educate her peers about these issues, La'Sandra co-wrote a newsletter with special online safety tips that she distributed at her high school.

Online Safety Tips

Follow these basic guidelines to make sure that all of your online experiences and friendships are safe and positive ones!

✳ Don't give out personal information such as your last name, your address, or your phone number. You wouldn't give that kind of information to a stranger on the street, so don't give it to a stranger online.

✳ If you have a bad feeling about something, ask for help. Is there an upsetting message in your inbox? Have you surfed your way onto a Web site that's giving you the creeps? Did someone say something confusing to you online? When you have a problem in life, your parents, guardians, and other trusted adults are there to help you and protect you. The same goes for online problems. Adults know how to handle this stuff, so don't try to go it alone.

* Never make plans to meet someone you don't know. Online buddies are not the same as your real-life friends. Lots of girls share their problems and give advice in chats and on message boards. When you get support from people on the Internet, it's pretty easy to feel close to them. That doesn't mean it's a good idea to take those online friendships offline. This can be a very dangerous situation. If an online buddy is asking to meet you, talk to your parents or another adult you trust.

* Don't believe everything you read or see online. Whether you're writing a paper or looking for photos of your favorite band, the Internet offers tons of information right at your fingertips. The problem is that not all of that information is 100 percent reliable or accurate. Visit the links sections of Web sites you like to see what they recommend. Trust your instincts. If something seems wrong, check with another source.

* Don't do anything online that costs money without asking your parents first. If there's something you want to buy, talk to a parent and get her or his permission.

* Keep your passwords private. Don't share your passwords with anyone except a parent, guardian, or trusted adult. Like the key to your diary, passwords are designed to protect your information and keep it for your eyes only.

Advice from Amazing Girls

Celebrate Your Friendships in Your Own Special Way!

"If someone is down, we do the 'goofy dance' around them to cheer them up!"

Tayler, 12

"The girls at my lunch table and I sit at the same place at lunch each day, except for one day a week and then we mix it up and switch places. On the day that we do switch places we do something fun like chip and dip day or decorate your own cookie day. It is really fun."

Natalie, 13

"My three best friends and I send each other a tie dye bandana during the summer and each one of us writes what we did during the time that we have it."

Lily, 11

"I'm actually new to a school but I met some awesome new friends and we've kind of started this thing where we make our own movies. For example we did our rendition of the *Blair Witch Project* and it was hilarious."

Leslie, 15

Journal It!

What is the most fun tradition you have with your friends?

_____

Is there a tradition you would like to start?

_____

Instant Messages

To: My BFFS

From: AmazingGirl101

The thing I love most about our friendship is

_____

Send!

To: A girl you would like to include in your supportive girls' community (who isn't a BFF)

From: AmazingGirl101

I'm trying to learn more about the girls at my school. Can you tell me something about your interests? Here's something about me (fill in with a fact you would like to share about yourself):

Send!

To: A trusted adult

From: AmzingGirl101

Who was your best friend when you were my age? Are you still friends with that person? How did your friendships change as you got older?

Send!

5 Crushes, Dating, and Relationships

Survey Says

* "A girl has to act like the girls on the TV or movies to be popular and fun and for the boys to like them."

  5th-grade girl

* "There is way too much pressure, especially from the media, to be skinny, popular, athletic, and have a boyfriend. Girls should be respected more as people than so-and-so's girlfriend."

  8th-grade girl

* "We are our own person and if given the right information will make the right choices."

  9th-grade girl

* 52 percent of girls say it is true that people think girls are only interested in love and romance.

* 39 percent of girls in middle school worry about sex and relationships.

* 28 percent of girls in middle school worry that they won't find a relationship.

* 21 percent of girls in middle school worry about being pressured to have sex.

* 13 percent of girls in middle school worry about getting AIDS.

* 8 percent of girls in middle school worry about getting pregnant before they are ready.

If you've ever had a crush on someone, you know that the word crush is a pretty accurate description of the experience! The first thing that can get crushed is your ability to concentrate on much of anything but when and where you're going to see or talk to that special someone. Before you know it, your thoughts and feelings get crushed together into one big "I heart (insert the object of your affection's name here)" mash-up. And if that person doesn't feel the same way about you? Well, that's when it can seem like your heart just might crush from the rejection.

From happily-ever-after fairy tales to reality TV hookups, girls grow up with lots of different messages about romance and dating. As you get older, all those love songs and love scenes start to take on a whole new meaning. Suddenly, you hear certain lyrics and it's as though every line sums up *exactly* how you feel about your crush. You see an onscreen kiss and you can instantly picture the face of the person *you* want to be locking lips with. And forget about trying to keep up with who's going out, who's breaking up, and who likes whom at your school. There's probably enough drama to fill a whole gossip magazine—and there are plenty of your classmates who would sign up for a subscription to get all the juicy details.

As you dive into the world of relationships, you'll also have questions. For starters, how can you tell if your crush is crushing on you? How do you know when you're ready to start dating? And what does dating *mean* exactly? How do you act? What do you do? It can be downright overwhelming to weigh all the hows and whats while your mind is spinning and your heart is racing. But through all the confusion, excitement, and disappointments (yep, *everyone* faces letdowns in the dating department), it's important to remember that you are, first and foremost, an amazing girl. Although there is no magic formula to make all of life's romances happy and heartbreak-free, amazing girls *do* have the power to make good decisions. And in the long run, your good decisions will get you a lot further in life than even the sweetest, sappiest soundtrack or the best, most Hollywood-worthy slow dance!

The Three Ts of Crushes, Dating, and Relationships

Whether you're already head over heels or just starting to think about dating, good relationship decisions start with these three Ts:

Truth

As your body changes and those hormones start raging, your head begins to buzz with questions. At the top of the list is the glaring need to know, "Am I normal?" OK, so some things you're thinking about might seem embarrassing, but we can assure you that you are not the first girl to wonder about them, and you definitely won't be the last! You have a right to accurate information when you need it and honest answers in a language you can understand.

Trust

You're probably more likely to blab about your first kiss or most embarrassing dating disasters to your BFFs, but don't forget that adults have been there and done that, too. Despite their sometimes questionable taste in clothing and music, they do happen to have a lot of life experience under their belts! You are always entitled to support and respect from caring adults whom you can trust to help you make smart choices.

Tools

We're not just talking about hammers and wrenches when we say "tools." Relationship tools are the skills, savvy, and know-how you'll need to make good decisions and take charge of your physical and emotional health when you start dating.

Try This: Make Your Three Ts Go-to List

Fill out this list. Each section has three slots. If you can't think of three answers, just do the best you can. Try to put at least one answer in each section.

Truth

What are your top three sources for reliable, accurate information about crushes, dating, and relationships?

1. _____
2. _____
3. _____

Trust

Who are three adults you trust to answer your questions and support you? If you don't always feel comfortable going to your mom or dad, you should have other adults on your list. You might include a relative, a teacher, a coach, a family friend, or a counselor from your place of worship or community.

1. _____
2. _____
3. _____

Tools

What are three relationship resources and skills you need in order to make good decisions in your life? For example, girls need to know how to protect themselves from early pregnancy and disease, so you can add "pregnancy and disease prevention" on your list. It's also important for girls to know how to set boundaries and be true to themselves in their romantic relationships. Are those skills you would add? What other relationship skills and resources are important to you?

1. _____
2. _____
3. _____

To: The adults on your go-to list

From: AmazingGirl101

Subject: My Three Ts List

I just filled out my Three Ts (truth, trust, and tools) Go-to List to help me make good decisions about crushes, dating, and relationships. I added you as one of the adults I trust. Can we set a time to talk about my list? I might have some other questions, too.

Send!

We know it can be tough to talk about this stuff with adults. Hey, they might feel a little embarrassed, too. But even if it seems awkward, the most important thing to keep in mind is that you're communicating with people you trust! Pick a quiet, private time when you won't be interrupted, and use your Three Ts Go-to List as a guide to make the conversation flow. Did this activity spark any other questions or worries you have about dating? You can (and should!) talk about them with the adults on your list. You also can try these "door openers":

* "Did you ever feel weird or scared about growing up when you were my age? Did you have any questions?"

* "How do you know when you're 'in love'?"

* "What did your mom or dad tell you about crushes, dating, relationships, and sex when you were growing up?"

✳ "Did teens have sex when you were a teenager? When do you think girls are ready to begin having sex?"

Advice from Amazing Girls

Don't Waste Your Time Trying to Make Someone Like You

"I went out with this guy for like a month and then he broke up with me," says Julie, 14. "But I continued to follow him around in the hopes that he'd like me again. So I guess I've been in the stalker's place." It didn't take Julie long to realize that her behavior wasn't making her feel good about herself, and no guy was worth that kind of stress. "Sixth grade is when everything—emotionally and physically—started happening for me. It was a huge transition time. That experience taught me to go with the flow and not get too attached." Julie learned that there's plenty of time in life for true love and serious relationships, but no girl should waste even a minute trying to make someone like her.

Not Every Girl Has to Be Boy Crazy

Cryshawna, 18, grew up going to Girls Inc. of Winston-Salem, North Carolina. "I see a lot of girls in middle school who are boy crazy because they think that's how they're 'supposed' to be," she says. She thinks too many girls try to act older than their age or copy the kind of behavior they see in magazines or music videos. Her advice to all girls? "Go at *your* pace." Cryshawna got through her own middle school years by having honest talks with her mom through a Girls Inc. program called Growing Together. "It helped me to feel more comfortable talking about my body, and I really liked that I got to do a program with my mom." Cryshawna is such a strong believer in parent-daughter communication that she now assists in the program.

Quiz: Myth or Fact?

You might hear kids at school joke around about "players" and "sluts." And if you watch TV, listen to the radio, or read magazines, you're no stranger to phrases like "hooking up" and "hitting that." But what's the real deal behind all that talk? Take this quiz to find out if you can tell the difference between some myths and facts. Read each statement, then write in the answer you think is correct.

Myth or Fact?:

1. Generally, girls begin puberty earlier than boys. _____

2. Most students in middle school or junior high have had sexual intercourse. _____

3. A girl can get pregnant before she has started menstruating. _____

4. If a girl isn't going out by the time she's 16, something is wrong with her. _____

5. A girl cannot get pregnant the first time she has sexual intercourse. _____

6. Women always show signs and symptoms if they have a sexually transmitted disease. _____

7. All men prefer women with big breasts. _____

8. Masturbating causes a person to go crazy. _____

9. Having sex helps make a person more grown up. _____

10. Boys need sex more than girls do. _____

Answer Key

1. Fact. Most girls begin puberty one to two years earlier than boys, but boys do catch up.

2. Myth. Because of media and peer pressure, most girls think this is true, but it isn't. Actually, most tweens say no to sexual intercourse — which is definitely a smart decision. They might have relationships with someone they like romantically, but sexual intercourse doesn't have to be a part of that.

3. Fact. Yes, an egg can leave the ovary and get fertilized by a male's sperm even if a girl starts having intercourse before she starts having periods.

4. Myth. Not a chance! Girls get interested in dating at different times, and some girls have other things they're more interested in. Girls should do what feels right for them and not worry about keeping up with friends.

5. Myth. A girl can get pregnant the first time she has sex, and it definitely has happened!

6. Myth. Both males and females can have a sexually transmitted disease (STD) without showing any symptoms. STDs are diseases passed through sexual intercourse or other close sexual contact. Often girls and women do not show symptoms because their reproductive organs are inside their bodies. People who don't have symptoms can infect their partners, and infected women who don't get treatment can infect their babies at birth.

7. Myth. Some men prefer women with large breasts, some prefer women with small breasts, and some don't have a preference.

8. Myth. Masturbation is a normal part of sexual expression for most people, both male and female. It will not cause a person to go crazy or blind. Many people of all ages masturbate. Some people don't because it goes against their values or religious beliefs. You're normal if you do it, and you're normal if you don't.

9. Myth. Things like emotional maturity, graduating from school, getting a job, earning money and living independently are what determines when a person is really grown up. Having sex too early, especially if it leads to pregnancy or a sexually transmitted disease, can prevent girls from doing the very things that would make them *truly* grown up.

10. Myth. No way! Neither boys nor girls need sex to be healthy. It's normal for boys and girls to have sexual feelings, especially when they start having crushes and dating. However, it is important to make good decisions about what you do with those feelings. Having sexual intercourse at an early age can lead to guilt and stress—and often pregnancy and sexually transmitted diseases. For these reasons, it's best to wait until you are older to begin having sexual intercourse. Sex is important to both males and females, once they're old enough to handle the physical and emotional consequences. Parents and trusted adults should talk to young people about when is the right time to take this big step.

Were there any answers that surprised you? Hearing jokes and slang about all this stuff is one thing, but when you break it all down to just the facts, it can be a little cringe-inducing. You might have even felt yourself blushing through this quiz. If you did, that's OK. As an amazing girl, you won't always be cool, calm, and collected; you won't have all the answers, either. Talk to the adults you trust, even when you feel embarrassed. Remember that amazing girls take care of themselves—and that means you ask questions, express your feelings, and get the information you need to make smart decisions.

"How can I improve my appearance? I love this celebrity a lot. I want to see him sooo bad. I've got TONS of pictures and he's the main theme of my MySpace [page]. My friends think he's ugly and won't talk about him and my parents say he's just a crush and he'll pass by soon, but this is the real thing! I'm extremely jealous of his GF. I can't stop thinking about him!"

Angie, 14

"I like this boy at school. He really is cute, and I am PICKY about my guys. I don't even know WHY I like him so much. Today my friend asked him if he liked me (without me saying she could, I might add). He said no. But I don't want to believe it. I REALLY want him to like me, but I don't know how to tell him."

Brady, 13

? *Is There Something Wrong with Me?*

Does it seem like all the girls at school are caught up in their crushes on guys? Well, the truth is that not every girl is attracted to boys and not every boy is attracted to girls. There are heterosexual people (those who are attracted to the other sex), homosexual people (those who are attracted to the same sex), and bisexual people (those who are attracted to both sexes) in this world. At Girls Inc., we believe every girl is amazing, whatever her sexual orientation. You should never have to feel ashamed or pretend to be someone you're not.

When you first start to feel sexual attraction, it can be a pretty overwhelming rush of hormones. It's okay to feel confused or to be "questioning" your sexuality for a while. As long as you are getting the support and resources you need to make healthy decisions, you will figure out what's right for you. If you're not sure where to go for support, check out the Resources section in the back of this book.

Role Model Remedy: Strive for a Healthy Relationship—with Yourself

Stephanie Quilao is a blogger and an entrepreneur who works in Silicon Valley, California—home to some of the largest high-tech businesses in the world. But when she became a millionaire early in her career, Stephanie's big business success turned into a big personal breakdown—and then a breakthrough.

"Money doesn't change you or make people like you, but it does have a way of revealing issues and problems you might have been trying to avoid," Stephanie explains. She realized that her biggest issue was her perfectionism. "I was afraid of letting people see that I didn't know everything. As a result, I never asked for help and I made very bad decisions about my money." When things started falling apart financially, Stephanie's eyes were opened to how much her perfectionism had been holding her back—in ways that were much more damaging than losing her first fortune.

"Growing up, I always focused on how other people saw me. I dated guys and I would act the way I thought they wanted me to act. I didn't act like myself," she remembers. Stephanie also suffered from an eating disorder. She got treatment, but her perfectionism lingered. "When I was raped by a boyfriend, I kept that a secret for five years. After it happened, I didn't even tell my best friend. It was more important for me to maintain the 'perfect girl' image," she says. Instead of turning to her family and friends for support, Stephanie tried to stuff her feelings down and convince everyone that she had everything under control. But she didn't have things under control. All that pretending led her to relapse into her disordered eating.

After years of hiding her pain, Stephanie was finally able to open up and tell the truth. She went to counseling to get healthy again. "Up until that point, I lived in fear of other people judging me, but I learned that I was the one who was constantly judging myself, blaming myself, and never feeling good enough about myself."

Today, she writes about her personal experiences in the hopes that she can reach other girls and women who might be feeling alone.

Stephanie is aware that the issues she struggled to overcome are still affecting girls today. As a blogger, she spends most of her days surfing Web sites, so she knows how great it can be to connect with people online. That's a big part of her job! But there are some not-so-great online behaviors she worries about. "Girls are posting sexy pictures of themselves on MySpace and buying into the idea that the more friends they have on their page or the more guys who think their profile is cute, the better they will feel about themselves. Believe me, it just doesn't work that way," she warns. "In fact, the more time you spend trying to make others like you, the less time you spend being true to yourself."

How do you feel about the world of crushes, dating, and relationships?

_____

Do you feel the same way this year as you did last year?

_____

Have you ever done something to try to make someone like you or want to go out with you?

_____

How did you act?

_____

What happened?

_____

What makes you like someone in that way?

_____

What qualities are important to you?

_____

6 Talents

Survey Says

✳ "It's hard to be a leader or a powerful person in this day and age. People don't think girls can handle the responsibility and don't give it to those who want it and can handle it."

8th-grade girl

✳ 63 percent of girls say that they belong to a club or organization.

✳ 52 percent of middle school girls say that they are always bored.

✳ 45 percent of girls say that it is true that girls are told not to brag about things they do well.

✳ 35 percent of girls say that it is true that people don't think girls are good leaders.

✳ 22 percent of girls say that they worry about doing well at sports.

✳ 20 percent of girls say that they play on sports teams.

✳ 18 percent of girls say that they take lessons (karate, music, dance, etc.).

Think about the last time you had a "Wow, that's amazing!" moment. Was there an element of surprise, astonishment, or eye-popping disbelief? When something amazes you, it certainly isn't an ordinary occurrence. Sometimes your amazement comes from the feeling that you've stumbled upon something completely unexpected. Amazing talents are like that, too. What's really amazing is that you can discover, develop, and celebrate new ones each and every day!

It's great to have special opportunities to be in the spotlight. But let's face it: not all of your talents will be recognized with prizes, performances, or trophies. Life is not about awards ceremonies, anyway—it's about trying your best, trying new things, and having fun while you're at it!

Bragging Rights

Too often, girls think that they shouldn't talk about their talents for fear of other girls' getting the impression that they are too "conceited" or boys' not liking them because they are too smart or outgoing. It's time to turn that thinking around! There is nothing wrong with taking credit for being the amazing girl you are—as long as you are not putting anyone else down in the process. Amazing girls build each other up. When one girl's light glows, that doesn't mean another girl's gets dimmer. It's quite the opposite, actually. Letting your own talents, strengths, and accomplishments shine brightly will light the way for other girls to let theirs shine, too.

* "I'm a good cheerleader. It's fun and energetic."

  Julia, 11

* "I really enjoy soccer. I'm a mixture of a tomboy and a girly girl. I play piano. I like to help people. That's about it!"

  Elsie, 12

* "I am a nice person and I'm funny!"

  Brandi, 9

* "I actually aced math! I learned to not get frustrated, to break down every problem and fact and set it straight. Math is actually pretty cool."

Caroline, 13

* "I can eat a tomato plain!"

Hales, 10

* "I make bead crafts. It relieves stress, too."

Julia, 13

* "What makes me unique and amazing is my singing because I feel like I have a good singing voice and many other talents. I like singing on stage at Girls Inc. to express myself more than I do normally."

Bebe, 10

* "I'm good at Earth Science."

Lee, 14

Role Model Remedy: You Don't Have to Be a Celebrity to Make Your Mark in the World

Kendall Ciesemier founded Kids Caring 4 Kids (*www.kidscaring4kids. org*) at the age of eleven after seeing an episode of *The Oprah Winfrey Show* about the AIDS epidemic in Africa. She became passionate about encouraging other kids to donate their time and money to support children whose lives are affected by AIDS. As Kendall faced a liver transplant, she asked friends and relatives to make donations instead of sending her flowers or gifts. Today, Kids Caring 4 Kids has raised more than $600,000, and 14-year-old Kendall has set a new goal of raising $1 million! She was recently commended by Bill Clinton in front of her entire school and appeared with the former president on *Oprah*, the show that inspired her to start her organization!

All the public recognition has been great for raising awareness about her cause, but Kendall says that running the organization also has led her to appreciate her own talents and to set personal goals for herself. "It helped me to find out what I want to do with my life," she explains. "Because of this charity, I know what my dream job is. I want to be a talk show host because I love talking to people and helping people and inspiring them to do something."

Having met some of her biggest heroes (aside from Oprah and Bill Clinton, she also has been introduced to Hilary Duff, Andre Agassi, and Bono), Kendall now has a realistic perspective on fame and celebrity. "A lot of times girls look at celebrities and they build them up so much in their heads," she says. "I met Hilary Duff in fifth grade. I was in her fan club, and I had her posters and CDs. It was a huge thrill because I got to hang out with her on set. But I also realized that you can't take a person and hold them up as more than they are. Hilary was really cool and nice, and it was an awesome experience, but she's just a person."

When Kendall put her personal passion into action, she not only made a huge difference in the lives of countless children in need, she also got to know some important things about herself. "If *you* know what's great about you, that's much more meaningful than random people knowing your name or recognizing you on the street," she says.

Kendall's Amazing Qualities

Understanding and empathetic. "I know what it means to go through hard things because I've been through hard times in my life."

Determined. "I'm the girl who's always trying to improve. I enjoy life way more when I'm doing things and taking risks even if I'm not the best."

Outgoing and friendly. "When I'm 100 percent real in myself, more people like that. I have no problem going up and talking to other girls who I might not be friends with."

What amazing talents and traits are you proud of?

_____

_____

_____

What is an amazing talent (or talents—don't hold back if there's more than one!) that you've discovered in the last year and that you didn't even know you had?

_____

Describe a time when you were embarrassed to "brag" about your amazing talent or a time when you kept quiet about one of your strengths or accomplishments.

_____

What did you learn from that experience?

_____

Try This: Make Your Best Book

You can't always be the best, but you can always try your best. A Best Book is like a scrapbook, in which you keep track of all the goals you've met and the accomplishments you are proud of—no matter how big or how small. Did you make a funny joke that cheered someone up? Did you study hard for a test and get a good grade? Did you overcome your nervousness and join a school club or try out for a sports team? Record it all in your Best Book! You can include writing, photos, drawings, and other items. Encourage your friends to keep Best Books, too. Consider hosting some amazing-girl bragging sessions. Get together to show off your books and talk about your goals and how you would like to fill the remaining empty pages!

Advice from Amazing Girls: Don't Limit Yourself

If your dream is to join the WNBA, you probably spend a big chunk of your time at basketball practice. And if you have hopes of becoming a professional photographer, you will focus your camera lens on that goal. But Meggie, 13, feels that girls should dream big and explore a variety of talents. "My talents are unique to me. I love writing fictional stories and I am good at it too. I won a writing contest for my local library twice," Meggie says. Her love of writing might lead Meggie to a career as a journalist or a writer, but she also has other talents and dreams about becoming a biologist, acting on stage, and even solving mysteries! "I am good at history and science," she says. "I made it to my school's drama club. I love to act and be funny. I am also sneaky, which makes me a good spy. I love forensic science and to be a spy, you must learn that. I enjoy using high technology to help me find clues and solve mysteries. Solving mysteries is important to the world because the world has more questions than answers." One of the great things about being a girl is that you don't need to have everything figured out. Meggie is having a good time exploring lots of amazing skills and talents.

Your Leadership Skills Checklist

Your talents, skills, and amazing qualities are all great ingredients for leadership! Being a good leader is about using your voice, expressing your feelings, and exercising your right to speak up. Check off the skills you have already put into action, and refer back to this list so you can check off more items as you accomplish them!

- ○ I've led an activity in a group, school, or club.
- ○ I've worked in a group to make a decision.
- ○ I've explained my ideas to someone.
- ○ I've used the library to do research.
- ○ I've used the computer to do research or send a message.
- ○ I've interviewed someone.

- ○ I've made a presentation to a group or in front of a class.
- ○ I've listened to others in both small and large groups.
- ○ I've learned new words.
- ○ I've written a letter to ask for something (for example: you could write a letter inviting a community leader to a meeting or requesting information for a report you're working on).
- ○ I've called local community leaders to support an issue or program I care about.
- ○ I've introduced myself to someone from a different neighborhood, city, or country.
- ○ I've gone out of my way for someone in trouble.
- ○ I've helped someone else meet her goals.
- ○ I've done something a little bit scary but important for me to do.
- ○ I've made a decision within my group of friends.
- ○ I've talked with others in my community about my concerns.
- ○ I've found other people to work with me to make a change.
- ○ I've made up a game or activity for a group.
- ○ I've made up a story or song and shared it with a group.
- ○ I've kept a journal.
- ○ I've written a song, poem, or story; made a picture; or created some object about girls and women—and connected it to an issue I care about in my own life. I've thought about the things that are hard for me to do and the things that are easy.

✉ *Instant Messages*

To: Your friends

From: AmazingGirl101

Subject: You're Amazing!

I want you to know that I think you're amazing! Here are just three of your amazing qualities:

_____   _____   _____

Send!

To: An adult you trust

From: AmazingGirl101

Subject: Shining Moment

I might not always be the best, but I try my best. An amazing moment when I felt really proud of myself was:

_____

Send!

To: An adult you trust

From: AmazingGirl101

Subject: The Road to Success

What would you say is your greatest success? What were the risks involved in pursuing that goal? What is your personal definition of success?

Send!

Role Model Remedy: Find the Courage to Believe in Your Incredible-ness!

Bonnie St. John is a successful businesswoman, a Rhodes Scholar (one of the most prestigious scholarships in the world), an author, an Olympic ski champion, and a former member of Girls Inc.! Bonnie faced many challenges growing up. And for a while, she believed her challenges were limitations. "I had a brace and orthopedic shoes up until the age of five, when I had my right foot amputated," Bonnie explains. "Growing up, I was 'the handicapped kid.' I even had a special bus that took me to school. I would never have dreamed of trying out for a sports team."

But all that changed when a friend invited Bonnie to go skiing for a week. "I accepted the invitation, but that meant I had to look for the special equipment I needed. I ended up finding a whole group of amputees who skied," she says. "I thought, 'This is great. I can race!' It opened a door to a whole other world for me. I had never seen competitive sports as an option before." Bonnie swung that door wide open as she climbed the competitive ranks and went on to win a silver medal in the Paralympics!

Bonnie has learned that life is full of those doors. Unfortunately, if you believe you can't open them because you're not perfect enough, you'll miss out on valuable opportunities to discover and develop your talents. "It takes courage to go after what you want. Certainly as the one-legged African-American girl from a not-so-rich family at the private school, not everybody was convinced that I was so incredible. But I believed I was, despite my differences and 'imperfections.' Every girl has to find the strength to take whatever she's got and find the incredible-ness of it."

7 Family

Survey Says

* "I think a lot of girl problems wouldn't arise if the parents took their roles [seriously] and stood up to be the parents and not the friends."

   4th-grade girl

* "There are a lot of pressures and stereotypes to deal with to be who we want to be and at the same time live up to who you want us to be."

   6th-grade girl

* "It's very difficult because there is so much pressure to be perfect. The media puts pressure on us to be thin; parents put pressure on us to get good grades. We are supposed to be nice. . . . Sometimes it seems unbearable. We just want acceptance."

   8th-grade girl

* 87 percent of girls say that they get along well with their parents.

* 50 percent of girls say it is true that girls are expected to spend a lot of their time on housework and taking care of younger sisters and brothers.

* 30 percent of girls say that they worry about getting along with their parents.

Family can make you feel safe, loved, and understood. Your parents knew you before anyone else did. After all, they've witnessed practically every step of your life. They might have even been right there with a camera to document your first actual step (not to mention the other more embarrassing moments you wish had not been captured for all eternity). But as you get older and you start taking more steps on your own, there are sure to be some days when you feel that they don't understand you.

Growing up is about growing into the person *you* want to be. When you and your mom or dad disagree about what that person should do or how that person should act, things can get pretty unpleasant. Parents say that they want what's best for you, and they are telling the truth. Here's the catch: what *they* want and what *you* want might not always match up. You want to go out with your friends; they want you to babysit. You want more computer time; they want more studying time. You have your own version of how you can be an amazing girl, and they have theirs.

It's important to remember that disagreements are a part of life; you shouldn't go out of your way to avoid them. All parents and daughters disagree sometimes. That's a tried-and-true fact you can count on—so embrace it now, amazing girl! You always have a right to your own feelings and opinions. If you spend your whole life trying to avoid conflict and be "good" and "nice," you'll miss out on expressing yourself and being heard. On the other hand, if you yell at the top of your lungs, your parents definitely will hear you, but they might be too frustrated or angry to really *listen* to what you have to say. When you accept that family disagreements are unavoidable, you can start focusing on how to deal with them in a way that gets amazing results instead of slammed doors or the silent treatment!

Try This: Deal with These Dilemmas

Find a time when your mom or dad has a few minutes to do this activity with you. Can you work together to apply the problem-solving strategy to these three dilemmas?

Problem-Solving Strategy

Identify the Problem

Listen to what the other person is saying and what he or she wants. Say what you want using "I" statements. "I" statements start with "I," and they are a way of expressing yourself without insulting or questioning the other person. Instead of "You never let me go anywhere," say "I want to be able to go places with my friends."

Talk About Your Feelings

Take turns describing how this dilemma makes you feel. Try out those "I" statements.

Identify Possible Solutions

Each of you make a list of as many possible solutions as you can think of. Write them all down.

Eliminate Solutions That Won't Work for Either of You

It's time to compare your lists. Look at the solutions you came up with, and cross out the solutions that either of you can't live with.

Choose from One of the Remaining Solutions

What's left on your list? Talk about the remaining solutions, and agree on one that will work for both of you. It might not be the first choice for either of you, but it must be workable for both of you.

Dilemma #1: The Curfew

Daughter: Your parent has set a curfew for you—you must be in the house by 8:00 P.M. on weekdays and 9:00 P.M. on weekends. You feel this is totally unfair. You have two friends in your neighborhood, and you like to watch TV together—but the best shows don't even start until 8:00! You would like to stay out later.

Parent: You set a curfew for your daughter—8:00 P.M. weekdays and 9:00 P.M. weekends. She says this is unrealistic because she always has to be the first one to leave whenever her friends get together. You are concerned that homework won't get done, and you worry that you can't monitor what shows she and her friends are watching on TV.

How do you deal?

Dilemma #2: Choice of Friends

Daughter: You've started hanging out with some kids who are older than you. They've told you that you're mature for your age. Your new friends are really cool, although one of them sometimes smokes. Now your other friends seem immature. Your parents disapprove.

Parent: Your daughter has started hanging out with a group of teens, and you've seen at least one of them smoking. You disapprove of her spending so much time with older kids, although her new friends seem nice enough.

How do you deal?

Dilemma #3: The Party

Daughter: You're invited to a friend's party this Saturday. You know that boys and girls are invited and your crush will definitely be there. You were honest with your parents and expected that they would allow you to go. But your parents don't think you should, especially since you told them that your friend's 18-year-old brother will be in charge and her parents won't be home.

Parent: Your daughter wants to go to a party, and she told you that both boys and girls are invited. You also know that the party will be chaperoned by an 18-year-old, because the parents will be away. You don't think your daughter has any business going to a party without parents present, so you said no. Your daughter is very upset about this decision.

How do you deal?

Journal It!

Did any of the activity dilemmas remind you of a real-life dilemma you've had to deal with?

_____

_____

If you could go back, would you have handled that dilemma differently?

_____

What's your opinion of the problem-solving strategy?

_____

Can you think of some times when it could work in your life?

_____

_____

_____

Advice from Amazing Girls

Sharing a Room Is Sharing a Bond

Tamara, 14, loves her 16-year-old sister Lindsay. It can be a challenge to share your space with someone else, but Tamara says that bunking with her sister helped them both to understand and respect each other. "Before we got our own rooms two or three years ago, we shared a room," she says. "That made us close sisters, and if she ever needs anything, I'll always be there to help her, and I know she'll always help me." One of the things Tamara appreciates about her relationship with her sister is that even though they don't always see things the same way, they can get through arguments because they share a special bond. "She always makes me laugh about anything just to make me smile," Tamara says. "Sometimes we fight, but then like five minutes later we'll start talking again."

Talk About Body Critiques, Don't Take Them In

As part of a group activity, 18-year-old Madrianne was once challenged to write a letter to a body part. "I wrote a letter to my feet. I appreciate how useful they are. They take me places, and I love the way they feel when I walk in the grass," she says. Writing this letter also made Madrianne realize how hard it was to think about what she liked about her body—it was much easier to go straight for the negatives. "My mother really focused a lot on my weight in high school, and she would comment on what I looked like," she remembers. "I tried to ignore her, but I shouldn't have pushed it aside because it all built up. Now I see how much better I would have felt if I had told her why those comments bothered me, and how I wanted her to ask me about things like school and my friends—not my looks."

Having healthy conversations about body image with your family members is a good way to nourish your own self-esteem. Negative body talk is so much a part of our culture that sometimes even the people you love most (mothers, sisters—even brothers and dads) can get caught up in it. But amazing girls choose the more positive path. Here are some "door openers" to get the positive conversations started:

* "What do you love about your body?"

* "When was the last time your body helped you achieve something you were proud of (running a race, hiking to a hilltop, etc.)?"

* "What is your definition of beauty?"

Try This: How Well Do You Know Your Family?

Long before Will Smith was a multimillionaire and a movie star, he was a rapper known as The Fresh Prince. Way back in 1989, he won a GRAMMY Award for a song called "Parents Just Don't Understand." The video is filled with hilarious 1980s outfits, but the lyrics have stood the test of time. Why? Because people of every generation have had those moments when they wished their parents had more of a clue. Ask your parents if they remember that song. Then try this activity to see if you can come to some new understandings about each other.

How do you think your parent would answer these questions? Give it your best shot!

How would my parent answer?

* What is your favorite kind of music?

* What is your favorite television show?

* What is your favorite restaurant?

* How old were you when you started dating?

* Where did you meet my mother/father?

* What do you dislike most about your work?

* Who is your closest friend?

* Bonus: Write your own question and fill in the answer you think your parent would give!

_____

_____

_____

Give the following questions to a parent. Her/his challenge is to answer the questions the same way *you* would answer them!

How would my daughter answer?

* What is your favorite school subject?

* What is your favorite music group?

* What is your favorite television show?

* What is your favorite color?

* Who is your closest friend?

* What would you do with $50?

* What is one worry you have about growing up?

* What is one thing you look forward to about growing up?

* Bonus: Write your own question and fill in the answer you think your daughter would give!

_____

_____

_____

OK, now compare your answers and find out how you did! With today's hectic lifestyles, it can be hard to get to know our families as well as we might like. Don't feel bad if you didn't get everything right or your parent got some questions wrong. The whole point is to learn some new facts about your family. You can try these questions with other family members, too. Do you think you know everything there is to know about your sibling or your grandmother? How much do they know about you?

✏ Journal It!

What did you find most surprising about this activity?

_____

What are the things you and your parent seemed to know the most about each other?

_____

Why do you think that is the case?

_____

What are the things you and your parent seemed to know the least about each other?

_____

Why do you think that is the case?

_____

Role Model Remedy: Family Comes in Many Forms

Michelle Taveras was born in the Dominican Republic and moved to New York City when she was 7 years old. "I am the product of two distinct cultures—Latino and American," says Michelle. "My family is very close-knit, as we maintain our Dominican traditions and values. I have two amazing sisters who are truly my best friends and inspiration."

Michelle had the opportunity to experience many other cultural viewpoints when she was chosen to represent New York City girls at the Fourth World Conference on Women in Beijing, China. "Our Girls Inc. branch allowed us to compete nationally for the opportunity to go on this adventure, and I was completely awestruck when my essay was one of the two chosen in New York," she remembers.

In Beijing, Michelle met girls from all around the world. She also faced her fear of public speaking when she delivered a speech about how the media influence girls in the United States. Michelle says she was incredibly nervous. Her Girls Inc. "family" encouraged her to take a chance. When she stepped up to that microphone, she realized that everyone in the room was supporting her, too. "I think we grow when we step outside of our 'comfort zone.' We feel uncomfortable and vulnerable, and that's OK. It is only then that we are strong and bold enough to tackle our fears and evolve to our next level," Michelle says. "You don't have to physically change your comfort zone in order to embrace the Girls Inc. mantra. Every time you are scared to raise your hand in class but you do it anyway is a victory!"

After her trip to Beijing, Michelle went on to win a Girls Inc. scholarship. She graduated from Syracuse University and is now the executive director for Jason Wu, one of the fashion industry's rising-star designers.

In an industry like fashion, where so much emphasis is placed on looks, it is important to have a strong sense of inner confidence. Michelle says that she didn't always feel good about herself, but being a member of Girls Inc. helped to build her self-esteem. "Coming from the Bronx and Spanish Harlem, my idea of beauty has never been stick thin. We have always celebrated curves, so growing up, I had the opposite problem. I always thought I was too thin—'chicken legs' being the term of choice those days," she says. "My insecurities were so severe I never wore a bathing suit without a T-shirt over it, and all I wore were long jeans in the summertime (it got really hot!). My involvement in Girls Inc. helped me find a safe haven where it was acceptable to be exactly who I was; over time, it became easier for me to feel confident enough (at first within the Girls Inc. group and eventually outside of it), to stop focusing on what other people thought or whether I fit into a beauty mold."

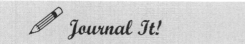

Journal It!

When you hear the word *family*, what words, people, and places come to mind?

_____

_____

_____

Tell Me

If you could tell your parents and other adults in your life one thing you need to hear from them to help you be a strong, smart, and bold girl, what would it be? Here's what some girls had to say!

✳ "Even if we make you angry or do something wrong, we always want to be told that we're loved and appreciated. Nobody's perfect."

Emma, 13

✳ "Respect our opinions and help us, don't control us!"

Tabitha, 12

✳ "Tell me I'm important!"

Rose, 11

✳ "That we can do anything. At school we always hear from our peers that we can't or don't know how to do something. To hear from an older figure that we CAN helps us feel like those others don't know what they're talking about."

Anne, 12

✳ "I need to know what you love about me. Too many people look only at my bad qualities, or tease me because I'm different."

Liz, 12

✳ "Tell me to always try my best, even when I'm scared."

Jade, 10

✉ *Instant Message*

To: Parents or other adults in your family

From: AmazingGirl101

Subject: Strong, Smart, and Bold

If I could choose one message I need to hear from you to help me be strong, smart, and bold in my life, it would be:

_____

Send!

8 Tough Breaks

Survey Says

* "With so many pressures heaped upon us and so many expectations, it is hard to just be yourself."

   10th-grade girl

* 73 percent of middle school girls say that they worry about achievement.

* 58 percent of middle school girls say that they worry about being teased or made fun of.

* 28 percent of girls worry about whether other people think they are cool.

You goofed up. You didn't make the team. You got a bad grade. You said something silly and embarrassed yourself in front of your crush. Or maybe you hurt your friend's feelings and set off an ugly drama that now seems impossible to repair. Most girls will experience one or all of those upsets in life. Tough breaks are, well, tough. But take heart because those disappointments don't have to derail you.

Amazing girls are not perfect. Heck, *no one* is perfect! Big news flash, right? Unfortunately, even though you might find yourself repeating that very logical truth in your head during those very cringe-worthy moments, it doesn't always take the sting out of your mistakes. One thing that usually *does* help is knowing that other girls can relate. Those "most embarrassing moments" magazine columns are popular for a reason—and it's not because girls take some twisted pleasure in reading about one another's humiliation. Nope, you turn to those terrible tales because every girl has had her own share of awful, stomach-sinking experiences. It's comforting to know that others have lived to tell about theirs. You will live through yours, too. And if you want to live your life to its fullest and be the best you can be, you'll have to embrace the fact that you are amazing regardless of whether you're playing your A game or not. Every time you "fail" at something, it also means you tried. Go ahead: allow yourself a few minutes to indulge in a little pity party if you must, but don't linger there too long. Sometimes what you build up in your mind to be your biggest setback *ever* is actually an opportunity to take a gigantic leap forward!

If you spend all your time rehearsing for your "Look at Me—I'm Flawless" one-girl show and being frustrated that you just can't seem to get it exactly right, you'll miss out on a lot of chances to learn, grow, and have fun in your real (and yes, imperfect) life.

The Agony of Defeat and the Thrill of Being a Good Sport

"When I was playing goalie on my soccer team, I had a totally bad game, and let every goal in."

Ari, 10

"I was playing the championship game for my volleyball team and we were winning 14-13. I went up to spike the ball to win the game and the opposing team blocked my spike."

Sarah, 13

"In the first game of the soccer play-offs last year, I almost scored, but the ball barely hit the top left corner where the two posts met. I can still remember that shot."

Marina, 11

Striking out is no picnic, but would you appreciate winning as much if you had no idea what it felt like to lose? Being a good sport in any competition means recognizing that losing doesn't make you a loser. The more you can learn about yourself from those tough breaks, the more of a winner you will be in life. Remember: there is plenty of fun and friendship to enjoy even when you're not #1!

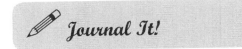 **Journal It!**

When was the last time you were challenged to be a good sport?

_____

How did you react?

_____

What did you learn?

_____

Sometimes the skills, good times, and relationships you "win" when you are part of a team or a competition are way more valuable than any championship or award. What have *you* won from being part of a team or a group competition?

Try This: Your Amazing Inner Light

Accomplishments don't define you, and neither do defeats—your inner qualities are what really make you amazing. Many girls say that they feel pressure from their parents to be the smartest, prettiest, or most talented. It's hard enough when you have to deal with self-doubt, but it's even worse when you're also worrying about your parents' being disappointed in you. So the next time you have a tough break, build yourself back up again by inviting your mom or dad or another adult who is important to you to help you celebrate your Amazing Inner Light.

Here's how it works: plan a shopping trip to pick out a candle with a scent, color, or design that's meaningful to you. Choose the inner talents and traits you want your candle to represent, and talk to your parent about why you picked those qualities. Then ask your parent if he or she has any qualities to add to your list.

When you have one of those no-good, will-I-ever-recover-from-this days, get out the candle and take a few minutes so you and your parent can light it together. As you watch the candle burn, picture your amazing qualities shining brightly within you. The flame still flickers even though you lost that game, got into an argument, or made a mistake, doesn't it? Your amazing light is still shining, too.

*Safety alert: Your Amazing Light is powerful, so please be careful! Never leave your candle unattended, and keep it far away from flammable items.

Role Model Remedy: Listen to What Your Mistakes Tell You

Jessica Weiner is an author and speaker who is also known as the "Queen of Self-Esteem." She has traveled all around the world talking to girls about self-esteem issues, but many years ago one of her biggest mistakes taught her the importance of listening.

Jessica was running a theater company when the Columbine High School shootings happened in 1999. To respond to the tragedy, she and her actors performed a play about the life of a school shooter for an audience of students in Jefferson County, Colorado, where the shootings took place. It did not go over well.

"People were booing and heckling. It was so bad, and I was in the middle of it," Jessica remembers. "I was facing 800 kids who were pissed off. I was so embarrassed that I was sick to [my] stomach." So how did she turn this disaster around? Jessica made a bold move and stopped the play in the middle of the production.

"I sat down on the edge of the stage with a microphone and said, 'OK, we suck. But why? What are we missing? How could we have made this better?' Kids started raising their hands and telling us what they thought, instead of us telling them about something we had never experienced. And that was the moment I realized how important it would be for me to be a good listener in my work," she says.

Jessica also discovered that if she really wanted to grow and learn from listening to others, she would have to find a way to quiet the judgmental voice inside her own head. "Believe it or not, an audience full of critics will never have the power to make me feel as bad as I can make myself feel," she says. Today, Jessica keeps that inner critic in check by living her life as an "Actionist."

"Whenever I find myself stuck in that perfection trap, what gets me out of it is taking action—whether it's going outside to take a walk, calling my mom, or making a to-do list," she says. "Every girl and woman needs to tell herself that there is plenty of success to go around! When we see the world through generous eyes, we will all be better for it. We have to first cut ourselves a break before anyone else will."

Trials, Errors, and Life Lessons

Want to know how you can get through a tough break without having a breakdown? Here's what some amazing role models told us about what they've gained from losing out, messing up, and falling on their faces!

> "When I was in high school, I tried out for the cheerleading team. During my tryout, I remember seeing the judges' faces and knowing right then and there that I wasn't going to make the team. I was disappointed, but deep down I think I knew in my soul that cheerleading was not for me. A couple years later I joined the mock-trial team, and I kicked butt!

I started a literary magazine, and that was a lot of fun, too. I just needed to find the activities that matched with what was in my heart."

Ann Shoket, editor-in-chief, *Seventeen* **magazine**

"My mom often tells the story of when I first learned to walk. I took a few steps, fell down, and broke out into a fit of giggles! Then I got up and did it again. For a whole day, it was just falling and giggling, over and over. As a baby, I had a blast taking all those tumbles, and that's the attitude I still live by. A few years ago, I signed up for windsurfing lessons. The instructor taught me how to fall in more ways than I could have ever imagined. It really took the pressure off because instead of focusing on the fear of falling, I could really get into the fun of learning."

Karen Salmansohn, author and motivational coach

"For a long time, I felt pressure to always do the 'right thing' and set a good example for my younger sister. But life is messy, and there really is no black-and-white definition of the 'right thing.' What's important is to do what's right for *you*. In order to follow your passions, you have to try different things. Mistakes are a natural part of that process. Now my goal is to make new mistakes every day. That's how I know I'm still growing as a person."

Simran Sethi, environmental activist and journalist

"I've never been much of an athlete, but I decided to join the cross-country team for fun. I was really slow, and I came in last in practically every race. Once I got over the fear of everyone laughing at me, I realized that people always cheer the hardest for the last person! My teammates were really supportive, and by end of the season, I got much better. There were even a couple of times when I didn't come in last."

Kendall Ciesemier, founder of Kids Caring 4 Kids

"Through the years, I've kept a journal. Along with my accomplishments and the things I'm proud of, I also record my fears and the mistakes I've made. It helps to express those feelings, and usually when I look back, I think, 'I can't believe I worried about that!' Honestly, I've learned much more from making mistakes and asking for help than I've ever learned from my successes."

Jean Otte, founder of WOMEN Unlimited

"Here's the big secret about perfection: people who try to be perfect are boring. They are! People's struggles are what are interesting. Think about it: you wouldn't have great artists or authors or musicians if they were all perfect—everyone writes about their challenges. Getting fired from my first job after college led me to the career I have now."

Hannah Seligson, career expert

Try This: Are You a Risk-Taker?

The Girls Inc. Girls' Bill of Rights[SM] states that "girls have the right to take risks, to strive feely, and to take pride in success." Sometimes it pays to take chances. Healthy risk-taking is one of the best ways to discover your amazing potential. Take this quiz to find out if you are a healthy risk-taker.

1. You and Tamara have been paired up as partners in your science class, and you've gotten to know her pretty well over the last few weeks. She can come across as a little hyper sometimes, but she's nice and likes a lot of the same music as you. You're thinking of inviting her to your upcoming birthday party, but you know that your best friends don't really like her. You definitely don't want any drama or hurt feelings at your party. What do you do?

   a. You invite Tamara. And while you're at it, you tell your friends that even though they might not like her, you do. If they're your true friends, they should respect your choice to include her.

   b. You invite her, but you end up stressing about whether your friends will give you a hard time about it. And then you stress some more about whether Tamara will get teased at the party, which would totally ruin your birthday fun.

   c. You don't invite her and spend the weeks leading up to your party trying to avoid mentioning anything birthday-related every time you see her.

2. Your English teacher asks the class a question about grammar. The topic was covered in last night's homework assignment, and you're pretty sure that you know the right answer—but not 100 percent. What do you do?

   a. Your hand goes straight up. You manage to refrain from shouting "Ooh, ooh, over here!" but you are hoping she calls on you.

   b. You hesitate, survey the room to see what the other kids are doing, then put your hand halfway up. It's probably better if she calls on someone who's sure about the answer, anyway.

   c. You start taking notes, shuffling your papers, or pretending that you're looking for something in your backpack. You are an expert at avoiding that dreaded possibility of giving a wrong answer in front of the entire class.

3. All of your friends are super excited about trying out for the school play. You're more interested in the new swim team starting up at your local recreation center. You love swimming, and you've never had the chance to be on a team. But there's no way you can manage both the play and the swim team. You will have to choose. What do you do?

   a. You join the swim team. You're passionate about swimming, so why not? Plus this will be a chance to meet some new friends who share that passion!

   b. You join the swim team, and you try out for the play, too. Even though you know you'll probably have to drop out if you get a part, you'll deal with that when or if you have to. You don't want to miss out on something all your friends seem so into.

   c. You try out for the play and try to forget about the swim team. You would rather do an activity with friends you know than go out on your own to do something where you won't know anyone.

4. Jamie, a girl from one of the popular cliques, lets you in on a joke that she and her friends have started. For the past few weeks, they've been making fake MySpace pages, pretending to be some of the not-so-popular kids in the class. Jamie gives you the passwords and asks you to join in because she likes your sense of humor. You

start logging on and posting silly messages. But when you hear that one of the girls you've been playing the joke on had to go to the guidance counselor because she's been crying a lot at school, you feel really bad. You'll get in big trouble if your parents find out what you've been up to online. What do you do?

a. You tell your parents. They'll be mad, but this whole situation has spun way out of control. Now you know it was a big mistake to have gotten involved in the first place, and you need help to figure out how to handle it. Jamie probably will be furious, too, but you figure it's better to take responsibility and face the consequences than to keep it quiet and continue feeling guilty.

b. You tell Jamie that you don't want to be part of the joke anymore. She and the other girls keep going with it, but you feel a little better about yourself knowing that you're not involved.

c. You stay quiet. You stop logging on and hope that no one finds out you have the passwords. When Jamie and her friends mention the joke at school, you still laugh along.

5. The last time you went to visit your cousin, she took you shopping at her favorite thrift store. You bought a wild-looking shirt with a fun retro pattern. It's not like anything else in your wardrobe and certainly not like anything you could find at the mall, but you love it. Where do you wear your new shirt?

a. Anywhere and everywhere! Who cares if it's not the height of fashion? You're all about making a bold statement with your style.

b. You save the shirt for occasions when you're just around your family or close friends. You like wearing it, but it's not in your party-outfit rotation.

c. You don't wear the shirt very much at all. Even though you like it, you're not convinced that anyone else will. And the last thing you need is to be called a fashion "don't."

Answer Key

Mostly As

You're not one to worry endlessly about making mistakes. Sometimes you even enjoy the thrill of not knowing exactly how things will turn out. Keep facing those fears! Be sure to stay true to yourself and ask for help when you need it. As long as the risks you take don't endanger yourself or anyone else, your adventurous attitude will take you far in life.

Mostly Bs

You are cautious and careful, but you also know the value of stepping outside your comfort zone. You're not immune to butterflies, nerves, and the fear of failure. Hey, not many people are! Allow yourself to feel all those feelings, then forge ahead to take some chances. You'll just keep getting more and more amazing—whether you win or you lose!

Mostly Cs

If there's a possibility of failure, you would rather stay under the radar than go out on a limb. "Play it safe" is pretty much your motto. You're smart to stay out of harm's way, but there are plenty of risks that won't hurt you even though they seem scary. If you learn to separate the unhealthy risks from the healthy ones, you can still protect yourself and start taking some chances to challenge yourself!

✉ *Instant Message*

To: Friend

From: AmazingGirl101

Subject: Your Toughest Break

What's the toughest break you've had in your life so far? Tell me what you learned from it!

Send!

✎ Journal It!

What do you think is the difference between a safe risk and an unsafe risk? Write down some examples.

Safe risks:

_____

_____

_____

Unsafe risks:

_____

_____

_____

✉ Instant Message

To: A parent or other adult you trust

From: AmazingGirl101

Subject: Taking Risks

Here's a list I made of some risks I think are safe and some that aren't. From your own experience, what safe and unsafe risks would you add?

Send!

9 Priorities

Survey Says

✳ "There's too much pressure to look good, act good, do as you are told and not cause trouble. Be quiet and do house chores all the time."

5th-grade girl

✳ 64 percent of middle school girls say that they stress about not having time to do all the things they want to do.

✳ 60 percent of middle school girls say that they have too much homework.

✳ 60 percent of middle school girls say that they stress about having to take too many tests at school.

✳ 55 percent of middle school girls say that they stress about not being able to do everything their teachers want them to do.

✳ 54 percent of middle school girls say that they stress about not being able to do everything their parents want them to do.

✳ 50 percent of girls say it's true that girls are expected to spend a lot of their time on housework and taking care of younger brothers and sisters.

✳ 44 percent of girls stress about not being able to do everything their friends want them to do.

Is your schedule fully booked from the crack of dawn until bedtime? Girls today juggle school, clubs, sports, lessons, friends, family, plus lots of other activities. No wonder so many girls say that they feel stressed and overwhelmed! There are a limited number of hours in a day, and as much as you might wish you could keep going and going and going, girls don't run on batteries! You're human, and that means you can't do everything and be everything to everyone all the time.

Part of growing up is learning how to figure out your very own, personal, 100 percent *YOU* goals and priorities. Have you ever spent a lot of time and energy on something just because you thought it was what you were "supposed" to do? Or maybe you remember working really hard toward a goal, only to realize that it was someone else who wanted you to achieve it more than you did? Whether you're coping with pressure from the media or expectations from your teachers, friends, and family, one way to get in touch with what *YOU* care about is to turn up the volume of your inner voice so it doesn't get drowned out by all that other feedback.

Think about it: If you let media messages dictate your schedule, you would probably be applying lip gloss and pimple cream 24/7 and constantly primping in front of the mirror! Is your ultimate goal to have the shiniest pout in the history of womankind? Well, then go for it. However, we're guessing that since you are an amazing girl, there are quite a few other things you want to accomplish in your life, right?

It's not just the media who influence how you spend your time; your friends and family also play a role. If your BFF is into narrating her own play-by-plays of every conversation she has with her crush while you're more into listening to the play-by-plays of that night's baseball game, it doesn't mean either of you has to change—it just means you have different interests and priorities. And if your parents' desire for you to have a sparkling clean room and babysit your younger sibling clashes with your desire to curl up on your cluttered bed and read your new book in peace, you certainly would not be the first girl to face such a dilemma. Remember, even when your very logical explanation that uninterrupted reading time is crucial to your development as the next great children's novelist doesn't succeed in charming the parental units, you always have a right to express your own dreams—whatever they might be.

Clarifying your priorities and goals can help you organize your time and keep a balanced focus on the things that are important to you. You'll find that as you get older, some will change and some will remain the same. Certain goals and priorities might move up your list, while some might drop off completely—and there will surely be lots of new ones to add as you discover more and more about yourself!

When you're super busy, it can seem impossible to squeeze in everything you want to accomplish. But no matter how hectic life gets, taking good care of yourself should always be a top priority. That doesn't mean you're selfish—it means you're doing exactly what it takes to be amazing! Because if you're happy and healthy, you'll be better prepared to tackle all those other things on your list.

Try This: What's Most Important to You?

Make a list of your top ten goals, with number one being the goal most important to you. You can use some suggestions from the Goals Box as a starting point and/or add your own specific goals. Remember to include a few of your short-term goals (what you want to accomplish now) and long-term goals (what you dream about for the future).

My Top Ten Goals

1. _____
2. _____
3. _____
4. _____
5. _____
6. _____
7. _____
8. _____
9. _____
10. _____

Goals Box

* ✳ Get good grades
* ✳ Win competitions or games
* ✳ Be a good friend
* ✳ Be a loving family member (daughter, granddaughter, sister, cousin, etc.)
* ✳ Feel healthy, confident, and happy
* ✳ Have pretty clothes and accessories
* ✳ Live my life according to my religion/faith
* ✳ Start dating
* ✳ Go to college
* ✳ Have an exciting career
* ✳ Make a difference in my community/in the world

Now make a list of the ten activities you spend your time doing during those hours when you're not at school or sleeping, with number one being your most time-consuming activity. You can use suggestions from the Activities Box and/or add your own.

My Top Ten Activities

1. _____
2. _____
3. _____
4. _____
5. _____
6. _____
7. _____
8. _____
9. _____
10. _____

Activities Box

* Spending time with family

* Hanging out with friends

* Studying/doing homework

* Babysitting

* Doing household chores

* Playing sports

* Taking lessons (music, karate, writing, etc.)

* Staying active/getting exercise

* Practicing my religion or faith

* Going online

* Relaxing and having fun

* Making myself look good

* Volunteering

Compare your goals and activities lists. Do you spend most of your time doing things that will help you accomplish your goals? For instance, if you put "feel healthy, confident, and happy" at the top of your goals list (and as we mentioned earlier, we think that's right where it belongs!), but "relaxing and having fun" is way at the bottom of your activities list, think about what prevents you from getting your goals and activities more in sync. What changes would you need to make in your schedule? Who could support you in making those changes?

It's also important to find balance. Just because you have a number-one goal, that doesn't mean that you should devote every waking hour toward achieving it. Your other goals deserve time and attention, too! And let's face it, some of the activities on your list might not rank so high or be there at all if not for your parents' input. You do have to respect your family's opinions, but you don't have to agree with them all the time. If your activities list is filled to the brim with their wishes and severely lacking your own wishes, talk to them and try to reach some compromises that will give you more time to follow the dreams that are most important to you.

Journal It!

How well do you think your personal goals match the activities you spend most of your time doing?

_____

What changes or adjustments would you like to make to the way you spend your time?

_____

What does the word *balance* mean to you when it comes to your goals and priorities? Do you think you have balance in your schedule?

Instant Message

To: My parents or other adults I trust

From: AmazingGirl101

- I made a list of my top ten goals and activities. Let's pick a time when I can share them with you. I want to get your advice and feedback!

Send!

Advice from Amazing Girls

Here's what other girls told us about their personal goals!

"One goal I have is to try not to make any enemies. I plan on doing this by being nice to everybody and not talking behind people's backs."

Ursula, 13

"I want to start participating in class and be more outgoing instead of just sitting around."

Amy, 11

"I want to learn Spanish."

Samantha, 9

"I want to get really good grades and not let the bullies bother me."

Rachel, 10

"My goal is to read more!"

Kimberly, 10

"Get a nice boyfriend and make As and Bs in school."

Ciara, 13

"I want to make new friends and find out what I am good at."

Zainab, 10

Role Model Remedy: Let Your Passions and Your Priorities Lead You

Addie Swartz has always been a go-getter. At the age of 12, she launched Addie's Apple Pies to earn money for a class trip to Spain. That enterprise lasted until it got so successful that her father, who was tired of seeing their house coated in flour, shut it down. But even though her first business venture got "downsized," her eagerness to develop ideas from her passions got a big boost. Addie went on to high school, college, business school, and jobs at companies including Disney and Reebok. She also became a mom, which gave her the idea to start her own company that would create positive messages for girls.

"I got my inspiration in, of all places, *the mall*," Addie says. "I was shopping with my eldest daughter and her friends one Friday night when we were confronted with a huge photo of an almost-naked woman just inside the door of Abercrombie & Fitch. The girls looked embarrassed. One of my daughter's friends said to her, 'Why do they have to do that?' Right then, I recognized the 'wake-up call.'"

As a mom, Addie's priority was to help her daughter keep her self-esteem going strong in a world where there is so much pressure to grow up fast, be pretty, perfect, and "sexy." As a businesswoman, she realized that lots of other girls might benefit from an alternative to overhyped and overexposed Britney, Paris, and Lindsay. So she started working to reach that goal.

A few years later, after taking the time to research her idea and find investors to fund it, Addie became the founder and CEO of B*tween Productions and the creator of the popular Beacon Street Girls® book series, which is read by girls across the globe!

Addie's Go-Getting Rules for Girls

1. **You gotta love it.**
    "Whatever you choose to do, make it something you feel passionate about, something that touches you personally. If it doesn't, it will be hard to overcome the hurdles that will come your way. Do what you believe in."

2. **Start from the heart.**
    "Look for opportunities right where you are, where you live. I have two daughters, who were my inspiration for starting the Beacon Street Girls. Remember that opportunity is right under your nose!"

3. **Talk it up!**
    "Talk to your parents, your teachers, your friends, and your friends' friends. Listen carefully to what they say. Almost everyone you meet can help you make your ideas better. It might sound uncomfortable, especially if you're shy, but when you're passionate about something (Rule #1), it comes more

naturally than you think. Ask for feedback along the way, too! It's important to stay connected."

4. **Never give up.**
   "When you make a mistake or face failure or rejection—*and you will*—pick yourself up and keep moving forward. I've had plenty of people turn me down or tell me that my goals are too hard or too risky. You just need to prove those naysayers wrong. I always say to myself, 'I'll show them!'"

5. **Be flexible.**
   "It's great to have a clear vision, but you have to be willing to adjust your goals as you grow and learn. If you stick too stubbornly to one fixed picture of what you want, you'll end up limiting what you can accomplish."

6. **Live in the moment.**
   "It's easy to get caught up in pushing for success and reaching your long-term goals. But sometimes you just have to stop and live in the moment. No matter what you're working toward, it will probably take longer than you expect, so it's important to take the time to enjoy what's happening along the way!"

Try This: Believe It, Achieve It!

Achieving any goal is a process. A plan of action can help keep you on track, and it's also a great way to mark all the amazing steps you take. You don't have to wait until you cross the finish line to give yourself credit for trying to get there!

Here's how it works:

1. Identify a realistic, achievable goal. We're not saying that you can't dream big dreams, but if your Believe It, Achieve It goal is to be the next *American Idol* and you've never sung a note in your life, then you're setting yourself up for unnecessary disappointment. A more helpful goal would be to try out for your school's chorus or to perform a song in front of an audience. You can work up

to the *American Idol* auditions from there if you're still interested! Think about the steps you need to take to reach that goal—for example, "research singing lessons," "find out more about local musical productions," "talk to other kids at school who are also interested in singing and performing," and "set aside time to practice and develop your skill."

2. Once you have your steps, get a blank piece of paper and create a plan of action that puts your steps into time intervals that you think you can manage: "Every week for one month, I will . . ."; "After two months, I will . . ."; and so on.

3. You can decorate your plan of action any way you like. If you think it will inspire you, consider hanging it on your door or on your bedroom wall. Or if you prefer, you can keep it simple and write the whole plan on notebook paper, fold it up, and put it away for a while. It's up to you!

4. Every time you succeed in taking a step on your plan, mark it with a star (draw it, sticker, glitter it, whatever!) and write these important words next to each achievement: "I'm Amazing!"

5. Celebrate! When you complete the steps and reach your goal, give yourself a big pat on the back, amazing girl! Enjoy the sense of accomplishment before you start creating your next plan. Think about what it was like to take each step and what you learned at each stage.

*Uh-oh. Sometimes plans of action stall, and sometimes they never get completed. If you make a plan and then have trouble seeing it through, it doesn't mean you're any less amazing. Goals can change, so maybe what was important to you when you started your plan doesn't seem as important anymore. Or maybe a step you thought you could do for an hour a night for a week needs to be adjusted to a half hour every other night for two weeks. It's OK to revise your plan, and it's also OK to call off the project entirely if you decide it doesn't feel like the right time to pursue that goal. You can always create a new plan to reach a new goal.

10 Stress

Survey Says

✳ "It's hard. We have to live up to what the adults in our lives expect from us, while dealing with peer pressure, while trying to decide who we are ourselves. So we are torn in three different directions. No wonder there is so much teen suicide and depression. We are trying to live up to three different areas in our lives."

9th-grade girl

✳ 60 percent of girls report that they often feel stressed.

✳ 33 percent of girls say that they often feel sad and unhappy.

✳ 25 percent of middle school girls say that they worry about being beaten up or attacked at school.

S-T-R-E-S-S. Most girls have experienced it and more than half of all girls say that they feel stressed a lot of the time. Stress isn't always a bad thing. Think about when you have butterflies in your stomach before you have to go on stage or run a race or when you're about to walk into a room where you don't know anyone. You might wish you could tame those jitters when they first wash over you, but you know that when that adrenaline starts pumping, things get moving. That's the kind of stress that can propel you toward new adventures. It certainly keeps life exciting!

And then there's the other kind of stress—the bad kind. It weighs heavily on your mind, body, and spirit, and it can do a real number on your confidence. Supergirls are experts when it comes to this stress because the pursuit of perfection is a guaranteed recipe for worry, anxiety, and tension. What's really sad is that the girls who try so hard to be the best, look the prettiest, and achieve the most are often the ones who end up getting overwhelmed to the point that they feel stuck in place or even that they're moving backward.

Supergirls are so focused on being perfect that when they're not perfect, they get stressed. Then they internalize all those bad feelings for fear of letting anyone know that they're stressed, because showing their stress would be a sign that they're not perfect. And pretending that things are A-OK when they are far from it is, well, stressful. Which leads to more insecurities about being imperfect. Are you following? We know, it's kind of exhausting to keep up. Essentially, supergirls are caught up in a loop that keeps piling more and more stress into their lives.

Athletes sometimes get what doctors call stress fractures, tiny cracks in the bone that happen when the muscles are so tired that they can't absorb the shock of the repeated impacts from running or jumping. Ouch! The supergirl stress loop might not lead to cracks in your bones, but all that stress on top of stress will wear you out and crack your self-esteem if you don't find healthy ways to deal with it.

So what do you do if you find yourself with a case of supergirl stress? Start with these stress-busting tips to turn it into some amazing-girl attitude!

Amazing-Girl Stress Busters

Reach out! When you feel stressed, don't keep it to yourself. Break that supergirl silence. Talk to your friends and the adults you trust. Contrary to what you might believe, "I'm not perfect," "I'm overwhelmed," "I need help," "I'm sad," and "I'm confused" are not phrases that make you weak. Actually, the better you get at saying them out loud, the stronger and more self-assured you will become!

Express your stress. Write in a journal, play music, go for a walk, pound your pillow, jump rope, do whatever you feel like doing to let out your frustrations. If you allow your emotions to build up inside you, you'll be more likely to feel overwhelmed, so try making stress-release activities a part of your daily schedule.

Check your health. When your body and mind are stressed and tired, you'll start feeling rundown, irritable, grouchy, and unable to concentrate. Stress makes you sick; being sick is stressful. There goes that whole supergirl stress loop again! It's important to make your health a priority. Protect yourself against stress with a strong mind and a strong body. Eat healthy foods, stay active, and get plenty of sleep every night.

Try This: Turn It Around

The stress girls experience often comes from others' expectations of how they should look and act and what they should accomplish. When supergirls fall short of those expectations, they get stressed because they let outside pressures affect what they believe about themselves. Amazing girls face disappointments and insecurities, too. But the difference is that amazing girls don't let others' expectations and criticisms wipe them out so much. With practice, you can learn to deflect that negativity and turn it around before it turns into bigtime stress!

Name the outside pressure in each of the following situations. Check off the turn-it-around tactics you would choose, and/or write in your own ideas. Then fill in your own "I'm amazing" affirmations to remind yourself that it's what *you* believe about yourself that matters most.

Situation #1: The Magazine

You and your friends are flipping through teen magazines, and each perfect model you see makes you feel more and more frustrated that you don't measure up. Your hair isn't that shiny, your stomach isn't that flat, and your clothes aren't stylish enough. You're getting stressed! Instead of thinking, "I'm not pretty enough!" or "I need to go on a diet, straighten my hair, clear up my skin, etc.," take a deep breath and turn it around!

It's not me, it's:

_____

Turn-It-Around Tactics—Which Tactics Would You Choose?

○ Write a letter to the magazine's editor. Explain how all those unrealistic, retouched images make you feel and ask for more images that reflect the kind of beauty you see in the amazing girls you know.

○ Ask your friends how all those perfect images make them feel. Vent about the pressures, and start a conversation about what real beauty means to each of you.

○ Shut the magazine and suggest that you and your friends do something different. Choose something that gets you moving, and think about how much you appreciate your body for what it can do, not just what it looks like.

Add Your Own Tactics

I'm amazing because:

_____

_____

_____

Situation #2: The Test

Your whole class has been preparing to take a big standardized test that is required by your state. You have to get a certain score in order to graduate, and your teachers have spent *a lot* of time going over the topics that will be covered. It's the night before the test, and you're getting stressed. Instead of thinking, "What will I do if I don't pass?" or "I don't think I studied hard enough!" take a deep breath and turn it around!

It's not me, it's

_____

Turn-It-Around Tactics—Which Tactics Would You Choose?

○ Put down the books and study guides and clear your mind with a relaxing activity you enjoy.

○ Eat a healthy dinner that makes you feel strong.

○ Start planning a fun "We survived!" activity that you and your friends can do together after the test is over.

Add Your Own Tactics

I'm amazing because:

_____

_____

_____

Situation #3: The Bully

There's a girl at school who has it out for you. She's called you a loser, told all the kids at school that you're gay, and now she's having a party and it seems as if practically everyone in the class is invited except for you. You've tried reasoning with her, but nothing works. You don't understand why she hates you so much, and you're getting stressed. Instead of thinking, "What's wrong with me?" or "What can I do to make her like me?" take a deep breath and turn it around!

It's not me, it's

_____

Turn-It-Around Tactics—Which Tactics Would You Choose?

- ○ Talk to your parents or another adult you trust about what's going on and how it makes you feel.

- ○ Find out if your school has any anti-bullying policies. Go to a teacher or a guidance counselor to discuss what resources are available to help you deal. (Our resources section also includes some good information.)

- ○ Get educated about bullying and the reasons why bullies do what they do.

Add Your Own Tactics

I'm amazing because:

_____

_____

_____

Role Model Remedy: Go Outside to Find Inner Peace

Simran Sethi is an award-winning journalist and one of the world's most recognized experts on living green and being environmentally conscious. Simran knows that having respect for nature isn't just good for the planet—it's good for your spirit. It can be a great stress reliever, too!

"I came to the United States as a baby, so I was raised to think of the world as a much bigger place than where I happened to be at any given moment," she says. "I was also lucky because my parents really educated me about the science of nature. When I asked them why the sky is blue, they gave me the facts! That taught me to really appreciate how incredible our earth is."

Simran's work and travel schedule can get hectic, but she says that her stress-relief routine is simple. "I look for health in the outside world," she says. "We see all these images of super-skinny women, but that's not real heath. Sometimes the best way to de-stress is to spend time outside. I used to live in Harlem, where I would hear diesel trucks going right by my apartment. But you can still find nature, even in a big city. I would go to the park or check out the farmers' market."

When you get caught up in your own daily stresses, Simran believes it can be very calming to step back and see yourself as part of a larger whole. "I call this idea 'my environment, my community, myself,'" she explains. "If you care about the nature around you, you're also caring about your community and taking care of yourself."

Advice from Amazing Girls

When your stress level feels as if it's through the roof, how do you deal? We asked some amazing girls to share their own stress-busting strategies!

* "I write a song about whatever problem I'm having."

  Malika, 12

* "Writing—it's the best thing ever!"

  Lisa, 12

* "I do scrapbooking and spend time with my dog."

  Gabrielle, 14

* "I like singing, dancing, and reading to calm myself."

  Lane, 11

✳ "I stretch or do yoga."

Meghan, 14

✳ "I take a long bath."

Carolina, 11

✳ "Playing piano is my way of relaxing."

Penelope, 14

✎ Journal It!

When was the last time you felt really stressed?

_____

How did you deal?

_____

Now try this free-writing exercise. Take out a watch with a second hand (or a digital timer) and give yourself 90 seconds to finish as many of the following sentences as you can. Don't worry about skipping some, and don't get hung up on spelling, grammar, or choosing just the right words. Let your thoughts go, and fill in the answers with whatever comes to your mind. Ready, set, write!

I am _____ .
I fear _____ .
I hope _____ .
I love _____ .
I wear _____ .
I eat _____ .
I try _____ .
I sleep _____ .

I feel _____ .

I read _____ .

I trust _____ .

I believe _____ .

I dream _____ .

I hate _____ .

I belong _____ .

I sing _____ .

I create _____ .

I need _____ .

I share _____ .

I support _____ .

My hair _____ .

My body _____ .

My friends _____ .

My family _____ .

My school _____ .

My room _____ .

My thoughts _____ .

✉ *Instant Message*

To: Your BFFs

From: AmazingGirl101

What is your best stress-busting tip? Here's mine:

_____

Send!

La'Sandra, 18, has one thing to say when she thinks about middle school: "It was so hard! That's the time of the big identity crisis, when you just want to be accepted." La'Sandra went through her share of trying to fit in with popular girls, and then she realized that the best thing she could do was surround herself with positive people who believed in her. "But every girl has some of that confusion, I think. Looking back, I would tell myself, 'You'll get through this! Things will get better.'"

When Stress Gets Dangerous

Some girls struggle with serious problems and unhealthy, life-threatening behaviors. Problems like these do not just go away on their own, and it's very important that if you or anyone you know fits these descriptions, you must talk to a trusted adult and get help. Of course, your friends are there for you, but some problems are too serious for girls to handle by themselves. If one of your friends comes to you with one of these issues, the best thing you can do for her is to go to an adult. And if you need support for yourself, it's OK to confide in your friends, but you have to talk to an adult, too.

We know it won't be easy. You might be afraid of getting yourself or someone else in trouble. You might think no one could really understand what you're dealing with. Or maybe your friend has sworn you to secrecy and you don't want to betray her trust. It's normal to feel all those things. But the bottom line is that you are an important part of a community of amazing girls—and you have a responsibility to take care of yourself and one another. That means having the courage to speak up when you or someone else is hurting. There are people who care about you and believe in you. You also will find a resource section in the back of this book that includes Web sites, books, and hotline numbers you can call for advice on how to deal with these issues. Remember that even when you feel your loneliest, you are never completely alone.

Depression

Depression is more than just the blues. Everyone feels down every once in a while, but if those feelings don't go away and a girl experiences a deeper, more intense sadness, it could be depression. Depression is an illness that affects the mind and the body; it can often lead to other dangerous behaviors such as alcohol and drug use, disordered eating, cutting, violence, and even suicide. Sometimes depression is triggered by certain events in a girl's life, but not always. Here are some signs and symptoms of depression:

* Feeling empty inside
* Feeling that there is nothing to look forward to in life
* Feeling irritable or annoyed all the time (as if the littlest thing could set you off at any minute)
* Not enjoying anything
* Losing interest in hanging out with your friends; spending more time alone
* Not being able to concentrate (your mind is constantly wandering all over the place)
* Sleeping too much or too little
* Crying a lot even if you don't know why you're crying
* Having less energy and feeling tired all the time
* Not eating enough and losing weight
* Eating too much and gaining weight
* Feeling guilty
* Getting stomach pains, headaches, or chest pain
* Thinking about death or suicide

If you recognize these signs and symptoms in yourself or in someone you know, please reach out to an adult. Don't keep it to yourself. Depression is treatable, and no one deserves to spend her life trapped in such a gray, unhappy place.

Suicidal Thoughts

Sadly, some girls get to a point when they feel that life is not worth living. According to the Centers for Disease Control and Prevention, suicide is the third leading cause of death among young people in the United States. When deep depression sets in, it can be hard to believe that life could ever get better. But no matter how hopeless you feel, suicide is never the answer. If you or someone you know has suicidal thoughts, don't keep it a secret. Talk to an adult who can help you, and if you're too afraid to do that, call one of the toll-free hotlines listed in the back of this book to talk to someone anonymously.

Disordered Eating

According to the National Eating Disorders Association, an estimated 10 million girls and women struggle with eating disorders such as anorexia and bulimia. Millions more have binge eating disorder. It's important to know that eating disorders aren't really about food and weight at all. People who struggle with eating disorders might be obsessed with size, but those are just surface symptoms of the pain they are feeling inside. What causes eating disorders? Well, most experts agree that there is a combination of factors to consider. Research shows that there are some biological reasons why certain people develop eating disorders. It's common for several people in the same family to have eating disorders although you might not be aware of this because sufferers are usually very secretive. Eating disorders are also linked to low self-esteem, depression, anxiety, and media messages that place so much emphasis on being thin.

If you've seen stories about eating disorders on TV or in magazines, chances are they were accompanied by pictures of very emaciated women with anorexia. Some girls and women do starve themselves to that point, but those pictures don't reflect what most eating disorders look like. Most of the time you wouldn't be able to tell that a person has an eating disorder just by looking at her or his (yes, boys and men get eating disorders, too) body shape. In fact, many people with eating disorders are an average weight or overweight. You don't have to be severely underweight to put your health at serious risk. Here are some signs and symptoms of eating disorders.

Anorexia

Anorexia is a potentially life-threatening eating disorder. People suffering with anorexia starve themselves.

Warning Signs of Anorexia

* Dramatic weight loss

* Thinking about weight, food, calories, fat grams, and dieting all the time

* Feeling "fat" or making comments about being overweight despite weight loss

* Feeling scared about gaining weight or being "fat"

* Denying hunger

* Making excuses to avoid mealtimes or situations involving food

* Feeling a need to "burn off" calories with a very strict exercise plan

* Withdrawing from your friends and the activities you used to enjoy.

Health Consequences of Anorexia

* Reduction of bone density (some girls and women with anorexia develop osteoporosis at a young age)

* Delay of puberty

* Loss of your period, if you've started menstruating

* Muscle loss and weakness

* Severe dehydration, which can lead to kidney failure

* Fainting, fatigue, and overall weakness

* Dry hair and skin and sometimes hair loss

* Heart failure

Bulimia

Bulimia also is life-threatening. People with bulimia binge (eat large amounts of food in a short amount of time, feeling as if they can't stop) and purge (force themselves to throw up after eating, over-exercise or do other things they mistakenly think will get rid of calories). None of these behaviors actually helps with weight loss, but each one can cause serious and life-threatening harm to a person's body.

Warning Signs of Bulimia

* Thinking about weight, food, calories, fat grams, and dieting all the time

* Unusual swelling of the cheeks or jaw area (chipmunk cheeks)

* Discoloration or staining of the teeth

* Withdrawing from your friends and the activities you used to enjoy

* Feeling out of control

* Feeling grouchy and irritable, with mood swings

Health Consequences of Bulimia

* Irregular heartbeats and possibly heart failure

* Inflammation and possible rupture of the esophagus

* Tooth decay and staining

* Chronic irregular bowel movements and constipation

Binge Eating Disorder / Compulsive Overeating

People with binge eating disorder eat lots of food in one sitting, and they feel that they can't stop. Unlike bulimics, binge eaters don't purge. Some people who are overweight or obese suffer from binge eating disorder.

Warning Signs of Binge Eating Disorder

* Feeling that you can't control your eating behavior

* Feeling ashamed or disgusted by your eating habits

* Eating when you're not hungry

* Eating in secret

Health Consequences of Binge Eating Disorder

* High blood pressure

* High cholesterol levels

* Heart disease

* Diabetes

* Gallbladder disease

Nowadays, it's almost expected that girls should be concerned about their weight, so it can be hard to recognize when things have gotten out of hand. Here's one simple question to ask yourself: are your worries about food and weight making it hard for you to enjoy your life and feel good about yourself? Are they affecting your schoolwork and your relationships with your family and friends? If the answer is yes, that's a problem. Many girls believe that losing weight will make them feel happier or that overeating is a way to escape their problems.

But if you're unhappy with yourself on the inside, trying to change how you look on the outside or numbing your feelings with food are not good solutions. You (or a someone you care about) might not have every symptom of anorexia, bulimia or binge eating disorder, but if you recognize a few of them, that's enough to reach out for help.

Alcohol/Substance Abuse

Girls who feel stress in their lives sometimes resort to alcohol, drugs, or smoking cigarettes as a way of coping or fitting in. If you've seen beer commercials on television, it sure looks like everyone is happy and having fun. But drinking, smoking, and doing drugs don't really relieve stress or anxiety, and they're not good confidence boosters, either. In fact, substance abuse actually creates more stress, and it can lead to serious health problems and very bad decisions. The peer pressure to try substances can be intense. Most kids who smoke or experiment with drugs or alcohol say that they do it because other kids are doing it and because they want to look cool.

Alcohol

Alcohol is a depressant. At first, drinking might give you a rush of confidence that makes you feel as if you're a more bubbly, outgoing version of your usual self. But drinking depresses the brain—it changes the way you think and speak, and it impairs your judgment. Girls who drink can end up saying things they don't mean, getting into fights, putting themselves in risky situations, or doing things they don't want to do.

Drinking also affects your body. In the short term, drinking alcohol can cause you to feel wobbly and dizzy, to slur your speech, or to throw up. People who drink too much can wake up feeling awful the next day (headache, upset stomach, general awfulness all around). In the long term, heavy drinking can damage the liver, the brain, and lead to other serious health problems and even death.

Drugs

Depression, stress, and other insecurities might lead girls to try drugs as a way of dealing or escaping. But just as with alcohol, the high from marijuana, cocaine, methamphetamines, ecstasy, crack, or heroin doesn't last long, and the lows keep getting lower as drug use progresses. And remember, drugs don't have to be illegal to cause serious harm. Some girls experiment with over-the-counter diet pills and powders to lose weight, and other girls use inhalants such as glue or paint to get high. Whether from a dealer or a drugstore, these drugs are dangerous for a girl's mind and body, and they can cause you to make unhealthy decisions, withdraw from life, and lose sight of your dreams.

Some girls experiment with drugs and alcohol, and they don't try it again until they're older—or they might never use alcohol or drugs again. Other girls get addicted to drinking and drug use, and it starts to affect their lives. Substance abuse can affect your schoolwork and your relationships with family and friends. It also puts girls at higher risk for pregnancy, sexual assault, sexually transmitted diseases, and suicide. Like eating disorders, substance abuse is an illness. If you are already feeling depressed, or if there is a history of alcoholism or drug abuse in your family, experimenting with alcohol or drugs could be an especially dangerous behavior for you. And if you or someone you know already has a drinking or drug problem, the sooner you reach out for help, the better your chances for getting back on the track to reaching your amazing goals.

Smoking

Have you ever heard someone say that she smokes because it helps her to relax? The truth is that people who smoke cigarettes might feel that smoking calms their nerves, but that's just part of the addiction. Actually, there's no scientific proof that smoking relieves stress. Although most kids who smoke say that they do it because they think it will make them cooler or have more friends, that is another giant myth. According to the National Institute on Drug Abuse, more than three-quarters of girls in eighth grade *disapprove* of smokers. And here's one more fact that girls are often confused about: smoking does not help you to lose weight. Replacing food with cigarettes is a bad idea all around. So there's really no good reason to smoke. Besides the risk of cancer, heart disease, emphysema, osteoporosis, and infertility in the long term, here are just a few of the reasons why smoking won't help any girl to feel better about herself or to feel less stressed out:

* Bad skin. Smoking constricts the blood vessels and prevents oxygen and nutrients from getting to your skin.

* Bad breath. Plain and simple, smoking makes your breath smell nasty. It can yellow your teeth, too.

* Stinky hair and clothes. The smell of stale smoke lingers in your hair and clothes. Yuck.

* Decreased athletic performance. Even if you have zero interest in team sports, every amazing girl needs to stay physically active to be healthy. Smoking will impair your breathing, decrease your energy level, and make it harder to exercise.

* Hard on your wallet. Smoking is expensive! And the money you spend on cigarettes will go up in smoke. Think about it: if you spend $6 a week on a pack of cigarettes, that adds up to more than $300 in just one year!

Cutting/Self-Injury

When life feels overwhelming or stressful, some girls resort to cutting, or injuring themselves. It can start as an impulse that seems impossible to resist. Girls who cut are looking for a way to relieve feelings they can't cope with—anger, anxiety, or pressure. Of course, the cut doesn't fix the root of a girl's problem—it only creates another wound. Like people with other types of addictions, people who start cutting feel that they can't stop. Cutters often have scars on their bodies, but their deepest pain is on the inside. Most cutters start the behavior between the ages of 10 and 16, so if you or someone you know is cutting herself, speak up and get some help. There are doctors and counselors who specialize in helping girls deal with these issues.

Violence and Abuse

Abuse in a girl's home or in her relationships can lead to stress, depression, and one or a combination of the other dangerous behaviors we've described in this chapter. It also can cause a girl to become violent, to join a gang, to bully other girls, or to get arrested. It is estimated that 40 to 70 percent of girls in the juvenile justice system have been physically or sexually abused.

Every girl has the right to feel safe in the world. Unfortunately, many girls don't.

* Nearly half of the households in which domestic violence occurs include at least one child under 12.

* Girls who are victims of sexual abuse are likely to experience the abuse in their homes, by someone they know.

* One in four girls reports wanting to leave her home because of abuse, whether or not she was the victim of the abuse.

* One in three high school girls reports experiencing some type of abuse (physical, sexual, or psychological) in her dating relationships.

Those statistics probably make you feel sad, but if you have experienced abuse, those numbers also should tell you that you are not alone. Lots of amazing girls and women know what it's like. Many girls also believe that they could have prevented the abuse if they had had acted differently, dressed differently, or said something in a different way. That's just not true. Abuse is never your fault. No one—whether a family member, boyfriend, or anyone else—has a right to hit you, touch you in a way that you don't want to be touched, or say things to you that make you feel worthless. Sometimes girls try to push down their feelings of shame, guilt, and anger when they're struggling to cope with an abusive situation. But when you keep abuse a secret, those feelings always come out in other painful ways. Speaking up is one of the hardest things you can do, and it takes a lot of courage. It's worth it, though, because staying silent will end up hurting you even more.

How Do I Help a Friend?

If one of your friends is struggling with a serious issue, here's what you can do:

* Amazing girls support each other, so give your friend a hug and tell her how much you care about her.

* Offer to go with your friend to talk to an adult if she's afraid to go on her own.

* If your friend hasn't admitted that she has a problem, but you've noticed lots of warning signs, confront her at a time when you can talk privately. Tell her in a clear and nonjudgmental way why you are worried. For example, if you think your friend is a cutter, you could say, "I've noticed some cuts and scars on your arms, and I'm worried about you. I'm here for you, and I think you need to talk to someone about this."

* If your friend swears you to secrecy or denies that there is a problem, explain to her that you care about her too much to keep this to yourself. She might get angry or upset, but in the long run, be confident in the knowledge that you are doing the right thing by going to an adult.

* Know your limitations. You can be there for your friend and help her to get support from a caring adult, but you can't fix your friend's problem. Girls who deal with these issues don't get better overnight, so it's important to be a kind and patient friend. Learn as much as you can about your friend's problem so you can be better prepared to support her.

What If Talking to an Adult Doesn't Help?

You need to talk to a trusted adult when stress gets serious and behavior gets dangerous. Unfortunately, adults sometimes can make mistakes and miss the mark when it comes to helping girls with big problems. Getting up the courage to talk to an adult is hard enough, but what if when you do, that adult doesn't believe you? Or what if she or he dismisses your problem or blows you off or doesn't listen to what you're really saying? If you get up the strength to confide in an adult and you end up feeling even worse, *do not give up*. Go to another adult. And if you don't get the support you need from that adult, go to another one or turn to the back of this book and call one of the hotline numbers. If you can't get through, call another number. The point is that if you don't find help on the first try, then go to option two, three, or four—or however many tries it takes. You are an amazing girl who deserves support and help from caring adults when you need it!

11 The Future

Survey Says

✳ "It is sometimes hard. I don't know what I'm supposed to be doing. I don't want to grow up because I think it's scary to be an adult."

4th-grade girl

✳ "I am only 9, let me decide what I want to do when I'm older."

3rd-grade girl

✳ "We don't want to just get married and have a baby and be stuck. We want to live our lives like anyone else, without people wanting us to be good cooks or cleaners or moms or babysitters. We can fight and travel and make lots of money and be a big part of the world if we weren't mostly stuck in the house raising kids and being told what to do."

4th-grade girl

✳ "Girls want their ideas respected. Girls want their future open to any dreams they might have."

3rd-grade girl

✳ 71 percent of girls aspire to go to college full time after high school.

✳ 38 percent of girls say it's true that most people think girls don't know how to take care of their own money.

✳ 37 percent of girls aspire to travel to exciting places after high school.

* 37 percent of girls say that they are worried that "college will be too expensive for me."

* 35 percent of girls say it's true that most people think the most important thing for girls is to get married and have children.

At the beginning of this book, we said that amazing girls can do anything—and it's true! The most exciting thing about the future is that it's wide open. There's no rule that says you have to accomplish everything today, tomorrow, or even twenty years from now. There are probably a few dreams you want to get started on right away, but for each one of those, there are so many other dreams you don't even know you have yet!

The world is full of possibilities for amazing girls—there's time to have fun, explore your interests, discover your passions, learn new things, make new friends, *and* make a difference. You don't need a detailed road map to tell you exactly what to do or where to go. As long as you get to know a little bit more about yourself each day, you can be sure you're headed in the right direction!

Try This: Make Your Crystal Ball

What do you see when you look into the future? Get creative and let your imagination take you on a journey! Name four places you might want to live one day. Think big! Choose at least one city that is outside the state where you live and one city that is outside the country where you live.

1. _____
2. _____
3. _____
4. _____

Now list four types of residences where you might like to live. Be as descriptive as you can be. If you love water, you might enjoy a beach house, a lake house, or even a houseboat. If you're into cities, perhaps a loft or a townhouse would suit you. Don't forget the details. How many rooms does each place have? Do you have a porch or a balcony? Would you build a dance floor or put a Ping-Pong table in the basement? Design your dream homes!

1. _____
2. _____
3. _____
4. _____

What are four careers that interest you? Get specific. If you want to be a scientist, think about what kind of scientist you might like to be. Do you want to find cures for diseases, study a particular kind of animal, or find out what's happening in outer space? Don't limit yourself! If you're pretty sure that you want to become an elementary school teacher, write that down as one option, plus choose a few other careers that might seem more wild or out there. Have you ever thought about what it might be like to be a racecar driver? Add some variety to your list!

1. _____
2. _____
3. _____
4. _____

Describe four different family arrangements that appeal to you. Remember, family doesn't mean you have to get married and have two kids. You can feel free to add that to your list if it matches your dreams, but family can be whatever you want it to be. It can be you and your dog or cat, it can be you and your friends, or it can be you and a partner with no kids. Think about what arrangements would make you feel happiest.

1. _____
2. _____
3. _____
4. _____

Finally, picture the kind of world in which you want to live. Are there things about the world that you would like to see changed in the future? What laws would exist? Would people treat one another differently from the way they treat one another today? Write down four of your visions for a brighter future and a happier world. With each vision, include an idea of how YOU can be part of making that vision become a reality.

1. _____
2. _____
3. _____
4. _____

Now it's time to make your crystal ball! Get a large piece of paper, and draw the outline of a crystal ball. Inside, you can write down your dreams from the lists, or you can make a collage using magazines, newspapers, or brochures. For instance, if you listed Hawaii as one of the places you might like to live, you could cut out a picture of a palm tree and paste it inside your crystal ball. When you're finished, keep your crystal ball in a safe place. It will be fun to go back and look at it someday!

Advice from Amazing Girls

Here's what real girls told us about their dreams for the future!

* "I want to be a famous artist and have a pug dog named Taffy."

  Bo, 9

* "I see myself at college taking classes to be a marine biologist."

  Rory, 10

* "I want to be an OB/GYN nurse that speaks Spanish fluently and knows sign language fluently."

  Khadijah, 13

* "I see myself owning my own zoo."

  Lulu, 12

* "I see myself in a nice house with a great husband. And I see me singing on stage."

  Natalie, 10

* "I want to be a guitarist!"

  Alannah, 12

* "My dream is to be a Chicana activist."

  Destiny, 11

* "I want to become the first female professional baseball player because baseball is my favorite sport!"

  Lindsey, 12

* "I would like to work in a law office, or maybe in politics, or working part-time for a catering business and acting. The coolest job for me is to be a Supreme Court Justice."

  Ellen, 13

✳ "My dream is to become President."

Misty, 11

✳ "I would go on a cruise around the world! That way I could visit everywhere."

Tiare, 14

✉ *Instant Message*

To: My BFF

From: AmazingGirl101

What are your amazing dreams for the future? Here are a few of mine:

_____

_____

_____

Send!

Role Model Remedy: Know Yourself, Shape the Future!

For a long time, 17-year-old Irene Young felt like the "token" Chinese girl at her school. Sometimes kids would call her names like "Spicy Asian Won Ton," or when they came over to her house, they would giggle about her mom's accent. "Granted, she does have a thick Chinese accent, but she's my mom! I love her," says Irene. "When people made comments about my mom in the past, I would feel really uncomfortable and even embarrassed. Then later on, I would feel horrible because I would realize that I should be defending her and our language and culture."

Irene struggled with her self-esteem through middle school and high school. But she started to understand that she was feeling bad about herself because she was internalizing a lot of negative comments from other people. They weren't just silly jokes—they were harmful and hurtful stereotypes! Irene also believed that even though she was the only Asian girl at her school, there were plenty of other girls at other schools who could relate to her experience, and she wanted to reach out and talk honestly about what she was going through. Irene was excited when she was chosen as one of four girls to participate in the Dove Reality Diaries, a six-week online series designed to give girls a self-esteem "reality check," that invited her to record video diaries about her life and post them for other girls around the world to watch and discuss. As she filmed each episode for the Reality Diaries, Irene was challenged to think about how the stereotypes she faced in her own life were really part of a larger problem—a problem that she could play a role in changing. "I was asked to make a collage, and at first I didn't even know how to go about doing it," Irene remembers. "So I just started to type words like 'Chinese,' 'Asian,' 'Chinese culture,' 'Chinese food,' 'Chinese people,' and 'Chinese media' into Internet search engines. Everything I included in my collage was part of the results that came from those searches. There were some images that weren't insulting or stereotypical, but I found for the most part that the search engines brought up images that were created to make fun of Chinese people."

Irene wanted to address the issue of stereotypes and labels in a way that helped her work through her own insecurities and raised awareness among her peers. An aspiring filmmaker, she decided to create a short film. "I felt really empowered while making, and especially finishing, my short film on labels," she says. "It doesn't deal with racial identity specifically, but it does address a lot of other labels and stereotypes. After all, labels aren't just racial in nature—they can also be words like 'marching band geek,' 'fattie,' 'jock,' 'princess,' etc. I really felt that I expressed myself and showed my perspective in the film, and that to me is really important."

Irene learned that she could take something painful and turn it into an opportunity to explore her own feelings, educate others, and do her part to make the future brighter for other girls. "I've opened up my eyes and the eyes of my peers to the impact of stereotypes," she says. "Many have already seen the film and viewed the collage, and I think there's somewhat of an understanding now between me and the community. I don't really feel like I'm expected to try to change myself and be more 'white' anymore. I feel like everyone is aware of who I am and now they realize they should respect me and my background. I know I definitely respect myself a lot more now."

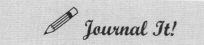

Journal It!

Think of a time when you felt angry or upset or experienced something unfair.

How do you think this issue might affect other girls?

_____

What are some ways that you could use your experience to change the world and shape the future?

_____

_____

_____

Instant Message

To: An adult I trust

From: AmazingGirl101

When you were my age, what were your dreams for the future? Did your dreams come true? How did they change?

Send!

Prince Charming Is for Fairy Tales

Princess books, clothes, movies, and dolls are all the rage these days. Lots of little girls have fun imagining magical lands and sparkly castles, but as you get older you start to realize that waiting for some dude on a white horse to show up and whisk you away is not really the best ticket to reaching your dreams. Sure, girls still want their share of mushy romance. But most of you say that in addition to loving relationships in which you're treated as an equal, you also want a good education and a cool career. The fact is that the majority of women will work for pay for most of their lives. Every girl needs to get ready to support herself, no matter where she goes or what she chooses to do in the future. At Girls Inc., we believe that girls have a right to prepare for interesting work and economic independence. So even if you're not earning a paycheck yet, you still can learn how to be a responsible money manager and a smart investor!

Try This: Your Dollars and Sense Checklist and Budget

Do you get an allowance? Have you ever earned money from babysitting or doing jobs in the neighborhood? Here are four basic concepts that are important when it comes to planning for your financial future: spending, saving, investing, and donating. Read the descriptions below, and check off which ones you already do with the money you earn.

Spend: This is what you do when you pay for something you need or want right now, such as clothes, music, lunch, or a movie. When you get older, you'll have responsibilities for more expenses, such as housing, utilities (heat and electricity), and insurance.

Save: This is what you do when you want to put away money for something that is very expensive, such as college, a car, a computer, or something unknown that you might need or want in the future. A savings account at a bank is the safest way to save money for a big expense.

Donate: This is what you do when you want to buy food for people or animals in need or give to a political or social organization that stands for what you believe in.

Invest: An example of investing your money is buying stock. Most of the companies that make the clothing you wear, the food you eat, and the items you use every day sell partial ownership of their companies in the form of "shares" of stock. When you buy shares of stock in a company, you become a shareholder. That means you will earn money if the company does well because you own a share of the profits. If the company is not successful, you will lose money because you own a share of the losses. Many people choose to invest in mutual funds that own shares in lots of companies. This is a way to spread out the risk of loss.

Budget

You probably don't have a problem spending your money, but unless you plan ahead and use your dollars *and* your sense, you might not spend wisely, or you might forget to save, donate, and invest some of your money. That's why it helps to have a budget.

It's your birthday! You just opened your card from Grandma, and there's $20 inside. What will you do with that money? Think about the things you want to buy now, the things you want to buy later, and the causes you would like to contribute to. How much will each of those things cost? Remember, it's always smart to save a little extra for unexpected needs and wants as well as things you're already planning to buy.

Write down the dollar amount you will spend and what you will spend it on. You must put some money in each category* and your total budget must add up to $20.

*Since most girls don't invest their money, we're leaving that category off this budget. But it's a good idea to learn more about investing so you can add it to your budget when you're older. Check out the Resources section for more information on the stock market.

Spend

Dollar amount:

What I will buy:

Save

Dollar amount:

What I am saving to buy:

Donate

Dollar amount:

The cause I am donating to:

Total = $20

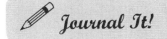

Journal It!

How did you decide how to divide up your $20?

_____

Was it easy or hard? Why?

_____

What did this activity help you decide about how to budget your money in the future?

_____

This budget required that you donate a dollar amount to a cause you care about.

Have you ever donated anything besides money to an organization?

_____

Have you done volunteer work?

_____

Describe what it felt like to contribute to a cause you care about it.

_____

To: A parent or other trusted adult

From: AmazingGirl101

I want to know more about spending, saving, investing, and donating. Does our family have a budget? How do you make decisions about what to spend, save, invest, and donate?

Send!

Advice from Amazing Girls:

Use Your Voice to Change the World for Girls!

Amazing girls are citizens of the world. They stand up and speak up on behalf of all girls.

Girls' Rights Week

Each spring, a group of Girls Inc. members from all over the United States comes together in Washington, D.C. for Girls Inc. Girls' Rights Week. They spend the week talking about the issues that matter to girls in their communities, and they meet with members of Congress to ask them to support girls' rights. La'Sandra, 18, had the opportunity to meet with Sheila Jackson Lee, a U.S. representative from Texas. She asked the congresswoman to support laws that would protect teens from dating violence, a problem that affects many girls in her community. Representative Jackson Lee commended La'Sandra for having the courage to speak out. "She told me that if you know in your gut you should be fighting for something, the right time to take action is *anytime*," La'Sandra remembers.

You don't have to travel to the capital to join this movement of girls! Every amazing girl can have a powerful influence on the people who make policies and laws. Write letters, send an e-mail, or call the offices of your senators, representatives, and local community leaders. Tell them what issues you care about, and share your own ideas on how to make the future brighter for all girls! If you need some tips on how to find their contact information, just turn to the "Instant-Messages Guide" in the back of this book.

Girls Study Girls Inc.

At Girls Inc. centers in California, Alabama, Kentucky, and Nebraska, teams of amazing girls set out to become investigators. They came up with their own questions, took photos, and conducted their own interviews to find out what Girls Inc. programs girls loved and what improvements could be made. At the end of the project, the teams presented their findings to influential community leaders with the power to make real changes! Girls explored everything from how Girls Inc. teaches members about personal hygiene to what programs could be improved to make Girls Inc. the hottest spot in town. Through their interviews, one of the teams from Girls Inc. of Omaha, Nebraska, learned that girls at their center wanted more science programs. After they gave their presentation, the staff started writing grants to get funding for the programs the girls requested!

🖉 *Journal It!*

Imagine that you are giving a presentation to make the case for changes that would benefit girls at your school or in your community.

How would you involve other girls in making your presentation?

_____

What points would you make?

_____

What changes would you request?

_____

What adults and peers would you invite to hear your presentation?

_____

_____

_____

Final Words . . . Amazing Beginnings

This is the end of the book, but it's just the beginning for you! You've got tons of new advice to follow and new tools to try. Have fun—and don't forget that as you go through life's ups and downs, the most important voice you can listen to is your own. We're not talking about that critical supergirl voice that puts you down and says that there's something terribly wrong with you when you fall short of perfection. She is so on the outs. That's right, say goodbye to her forever! You have a new voice now—a voice that tells you that mistakes will be tough but you will survive them, a voice that is not afraid to speak up for you and other girls, a voice that is strong, powerful, and, you guessed it, amazing.

✎ Journal It!

What do you think are the biggest differences between supergirls and amazing girls?

What supergirl behaviors or thoughts of *yours* are you going to turn into amazing-girl actions after reading this book?

Try This: Dear World

If you could send a message to the world about what it's like growing up as a girl today, what would your letter say?

Dear World,

_____

_____

_____

_____

_____

_____

_____

_____

_____

_____

_____

_____

_____

_____

_____

_____

_____

_____

_____

Signed,

_____

Instant-Messages Guide

Throughout this book, we have included "instant messages" that you can send to your friends, parents, teachers, and even community leaders and the media. Each message is designed to help you take your amazing ideas straight from the page right into your real life! Although you might not send all of these as actual instant messages, we're challenging you to start the communication just as quickly. Here are some ideas for how to hit "send." Depending on the content of your messages, you might want to use a combination of these delivery methods.

Parents or Other Adults You Trust

Electronically: If your parents have e-mail or IM or if they're savvy cell phone users, you can send your messages straight to their laptops and other portable devices.

Interactive instant-messages journal: Buy a blank notebook or journal and designate it as your "instant-messages journal." When you have a message for your parent, you can write it in the journal and leave it for him or her to read. Your parent can respond in writing on the next page and then return the journal to you. Sometimes things will come up that you might want to talk about in person, but starting things out in writing is a good way to take the pressure off if you're not sure how to broach the topic.

Instant-messages box: Similar to the journal, you and your parent can set up an "instant-messages box" in a common area in your house. When you have a message, write it on a piece of paper, address it to your parent, and drop it in. Your parent should check the box a few times a week. She or he can respond to your notes and drop the responses back in the box, where you can retrieve them. Some messages are sure to lead to face-to-face conversation, but this is another good way to kick off the communication. It also allows both of you to respond on your own time when you have the energy to devote to a thoughtful, respectful exchange.

The good old-fashioned art of conversation: If you and your mom or dad (or other adult you feel close to) are hanging out together, why not just talk about one or more of the instant messages while you're enjoying some quality time?

Friends/BFFs

Electronically: You and your friends might be *very* familiar with the world of IM and texting already. So go ahead and type in those screen names and numbers if that's what would be most fun for you.

Interactive instant-messages journal: You can create an instant-messages journal (like the one you share with your parents) to share with a BFF or a few of your close friends. Remember, your journal isn't a slam book or an excuse to be cliquey or to pass notes. It's a place for you to write and respond to the instant messages, questions, ideas, and inspiration in this book. Pass it back and forth as you fill in your answers.

The good old-fashioned art of conversation: Although computers and cell phones might have us all talking in LOLs and smileys by the year 2020, amazing girls do understand the value of girl talk (you know, that thing you do with your voice that doesn't involve a keypad or screen?)! So the next time you're hanging with your BFF, you can send her an instant message in the form of a question you ask out loud.

Teachers

Electronically: Some teachers allow their students to communicate with them by e-mail or through a blog or Web site. If this is an option, you can use it to send your instant messages.

Snail mail: Most schools give their teachers mailboxes, where they can receive notices and mail. You can write your message as a note to your teacher, then ask the receptionist in your school's main office to put the note in your teacher's mailbox.

The good old-fashioned art of conversation: A tried-and-true method, face-to-face conversation is the most "instant" way to get a response to your instant message. If you have time to stay for a few minutes before or after class, you can deliver your message in person. Or ask to set up an appointment. Get out your calendars and find a time that works for both of you.

The Media, Government Officials, and Community Leaders

Go to *www.girlsinc.org/ic* and click on "Take Action" and then on "Legislative Action Center." Click on "Elected Officials," "Issues and Legislation," or "Media Guide," and you'll find the contact information you will need to send letters or e-mails to your representatives in government as well as media influencers.

If you want to write to a magazine or a newspaper about a specific issue or send them one of the instant messages in this book, you can turn to "letters to the editor" of that publication to find the contact information and instructions on how to submit your letter.

Resources

Girls Inc.

Girls Inc.
120 Wall St.
Third Floor
New York, NY 10005
1-212-509-2000
www.girlsinc.org

Girls Inc. is a nonprofit organization that inspires all girls to be strong, smart, and bold. With local roots dating to 1864 and national status since 1945, Girls Inc. has responded to the changing needs of girls through research-based programs and advocacy that empower girls to reach their potential and to understand, value, and assert their rights.

To become a member of our online community just for girls, visit *www.girlsinc-online.org*. Connect with other girls, read more about inspiring role models, and try amazing games, quizzes, and activities.

To find out if there are Girls Inc. programs available in your community, visit *www.girlsinc.org*.

Girls Inc. Programs

Girls Inc. Economic Literacy®

Girls learn to manage money and invest, and begin to develop an appreciation for global economics.

Girls Inc. Friendly PEERsuasion®

Girls develop skills to resist pressure to use harmful substances such as alcohol, tobacco, household chemicals, and other drugs.

Girls Inc. Leadership and Community Action^{SM}

Girls build their leadership skills and create lasting social change through community action projects.

Girls Inc. Media Literacy®

Girls learn to analyze critically what they see and hear in the media; advocate for change in entertainment, news, and advertising media; and create images that are more realistic and reflective of their lives.

Girls Inc. Operation SMART®

Girls develop enthusiasm for and skills in science, technology, engineering, and mathematics, and consider careers in these fields by interacting with women and men pursuing such careers.

Girls Inc. Preventing Adolescent Pregnancy®

Girls acquire the knowledge and skills necessary to take charge of and to make informed, thoughtful decisions about their sexual health.

Girls Inc. Project BOLD®

Girls learn to lead safer lives by developing skills and strategies for self-defense, including physical techniques and the ability to seek out and talk to caring adults about personal-violence issues.

Girls Inc. Sporting Chance®

Girls learn to appreciate an active lifestyle as they develop movement and athletic skills, cooperative and competitive spirit, health awareness, and interest in sports and adventure.

General Health

KidsHealth and TeensHealth
www.kidshealth.org

KidsHealth and TeensHealth offer tons of great information on pretty much every topic related to your body and your mind. You can browse the articles or search by topic or keyword. Every article is reviewed by doctors and experts, so you know what you're reading is accurate.

Suicide, Depression, or Crisis

❱ Mental Health America
www.nmha.org

1-800-273-TALK

❱ CrisisLink
www.crisislink.org

1-800-SUICIDE

Abuse or Assault

❱ Childhelp National Child Abuse Hotline
www.childhelp.org

1-800-4-A-CHILD

❱ National Domestic Violence Hotline
www.ndvh.org

1-800-799-SAFE or 1-800-787-3224 (TTY)

❱ Rape, Abuse & Incest National Network
www.rainn.org

1-800-656-HOPE

In Love and in Danger: A Teen's Guide to Breaking Free of Abusive Relationships by Barrie Levy (Seal Press, 2006)

Eating Disorders

❱ National Eating Disorders Association

www.nationaleatingdisorders.org

1-800-931-2237

If you or someone you know is dealing with disordered eating or concerned about body-image issues, please visit the Web site or call the toll-free Helpline for advice and information.

❱ EDReferral.com

www.edreferral.com

You can visit this Web site and search for eating-disorder treatment and support groups in your area.

Stereotypes and Labels

❱ Gay, Lesbian and Straight Education Network

www.glsen.org

1-212-727-0135

❱ No Name-Calling Week

nonamecallingweek.org

Am I Blue?: Coming Out from the Silence edited by Marion Dane Bauer (HarperCollins, 1994)

This is a collection of short stories for young readers exploring the various meanings of gay/lesbian identity.

Boy V. Girl?: How Gender Shapes Who We Are, What We Want, and How We Get Along by George Abrahams, Ph.D., and Sheila Ahlbrand (Free Spirit Publishing, 2002)

More Than a Label: Why What You Wear or Who You're With Doesn't Define Who You Are by Aisha Muharrar (Free Spirit Publishing, 2002)

Body Image and the Media

❱ Campaign for Real Beauty

www.campaignforrealbeauty.com

Check out the Girls Only Interactive Self-Esteem Zone, where you can take self-esteem quizzes and test your media smarts.

❱ Inside Beauty

www.insidebeauty.org

This is the Web site of author Claire Mysko and Magali Amadei, the top model featured as a role model in this book. Read Magali and Claire's true-beauty tips for girls and women.

❱ Step Up Women's Network

www.suwn.org

Step Up Women's Network is a national non-profit membership organization dedicated to strengthening community resources for women and girls.

❱ With Jess

www.withjess.com

Here's another cool Web site from another one of our role models, Jess Weiner, aka "Queen of Self-Esteem."

All Made Up: A Girl's Guide to Seeing Through Celebrity Hype to Celebrate Real Beauty by Audrey D. Brashich; illustrated by Shawn Banner (Walker Books for Young Readers, 2006)

Crushes and Relationships

❱ Sex, Etc.

www.sexetc.org

This health and sexuality Web site written by teens is part of the Teen-to-Teen Sexuality Education Project developed by Answer, a leading national organization dedicated to providing and promoting comprehensive sexuality education.

It's Perfectly Normal: Changing Bodies, Growing Up, Sex & Sexual Health by Robie H. Harris; illustrated by Michael Emberley (Candlewick Press, 1994)

GLBTQ: The Survival Guide for Queer & Questioning Teens by Kelly Huegel (Free Spirit Publishing, 2003)

Leadership and Making a Difference

❱ NetAid

www.netaid.org

NetAid's mission is "educating, inspiring and empowering young people to fight global poverty."

❱ idealist.org

www.idealist.org

Click on "Kids & Teens" on the home page to find volunteer opportunities that match your passions!

❱ Kids Caring 4 Kids

www.kidscaring4kids.org

Get involved with the organization founded by Kendall Ciesemier, one of the role models featured in this book!

❱ The Democracy Project

www.pbskids.org/democracy

The Democracy Project has lots of information about government and elections. What kind of president would you be? Play the President for a Day game.

33 Things Every Girl Should Know About Women's History: From Suffragettes to Skirt Lengths to the E.R.A. edited by Tonya Bolden (Crown Publishers, 2002)

Bullying

❱ Stop Bullying Now!

www.stopbullyingnow.hrsa.gov

Take a stand. Lend a hand.

Just Kidding by Annie Bryant (B*tween Productions, 2007)

In this book, the Beacon Street Girls learn about cyber-bullying, gossip, no-jokes zones, and how the Internet can spread rumors, spoil friendships, and contribute to hurt feelings.

Economic Literacy and Money Management

❱ younginvestor.com

www.younginvestor.com

Invest it, earn it, plan it, play it!

Moneymakers: Good Cents for Girls by Ingrid Roper; illustrated by Susan Synarski (Pleasant Company Publications, 1998)

Other Great Resources for Girls

❱ Girl Power!

www.girlpower.gov

Developed by the U.S. Department of Health and Human Services, this Web site encourages girls to make the most of their lives.

❱ Go Girl World

www.gogirlworld.org

The Women's Sports Foundation created this sports and fitness Web site just for girls.

❱ New Moon magazine

www.newmoongirlmedia.com

This is a safe, ad-free resource for all girls who want their voices heard and their dreams taken seriously.

Respect: A Girl's Guide to Getting Respect & Dealing When Your Line Is Crossed by Courtney Macavinta and Andrea Vander Pluym (Free Spirit Publishing, 2005). You also can visit the author's Web site, Respect Rx (www.respectrx.com), for more tips.

Index

A

Abuse, advice for handling, 120–21

Action plan, for goals and priorities, 101–2

Activities, goals and fun and, 95–98

Adults
getting help from, 123
instant messages to, 11, 24, 46, 51–52, 66, 79, 91
ways to communicate with, 140–41

Advice, ix
crushes, dating, and relationships, 52
family, 73–74
friends, 39, 40–41, 43–45
future, 129–30, 136–37
looks and style, 22–23
priorities, 99
school, 29
stereotypes and labels, 7–8
stress, 109–10, 112
talents, 64

Alcohol abuse, 120

Amadei, Magali, 16

A-Maze-ing communication, 42

Amazing Inner Light, 84

Anorexia, 114–16

Arnoult, Duffy-Marie, 17–18

Assumptions, avoiding, 8

B

B*tween Productions, 100

Beacon Street Girls® book series, 100

Beauty. *See* Looks and style

Best Book idea, 63

Bill of Rights (of Girls' Inc.), vii, 31, 87

Binge eating disorder, 117–18

Bisexual people, 56

Body image, 73–74

Body Peace Project, 20–22

Bragging rights, 60–61

Budgeting skills, 132–36

Bulimia, 114, 116–17

Bully, handling stress from, 107–8

Buzzwords, about beauty, 18

C

Candle lighting idea, 84

Careers
stereotypes and, 8
thinking about your future, 127

Ciesemier, Kendall, 61–62, 86

City, thinking of future home in, 126

Communities of supportive girls, 38–39

stress, 105–8
talents, 63
tough breaks, 84, 87–90

V

Violence, 120–21

W

Wage gap, 3
Weiner, Jessica, 84–85
WOMEN Unlimited, 8–9
World
  thinking about your future,
    128
  message to about growing up
    today, 139

Y

Young, Irene, 130–32
Yurish, Jack, 9

About the Author

Claire Mysko grew up outside of Baltimore, then moved to New York at the age of seventeen to pursue her big city dreams (and go to college). She worked for several girls' Web sites, where she quickly mastered the correct uses of LOL, BRB, and TTYL. Claire writes about self-esteem and body image and has traveled the country talking to girls about these topics. She lives with her amazing husband in the coolest neighborhood in Brooklyn. Her site is *www.clairemysko.com.*